KT-234-636

DIANA LAMPLUGH

Diana Lamplugh is the mother of Suzy Lamplugh, the estate agent whose tragic disappearance while at work shocked the country. In response to this terrible event, Diana founded The Suzy Lamplugh Trust, in order to promote awareness of aggression in the workplace, and to protect the many other vulnerable working women from suffering Suzy's fate. So far, Diana has been highly successful. This book is the result of her hard-won experience, and an essential part of the work of the Trust.

Diana Lamplugh was born in Cheltenham. She is the co-founder of the British Slimnastics Association, and the author of many books in the Slimnastics series. She is married with three other children and lives in London.

00017015

BEATING AGGRESSION

BY THE SAME AUTHOR

with Pamela Nottidge
Slimnastics
The Commonsense Guide to Stress Control
The New Penguin Slimnastics – A Guide to Good Living
Slimnastics – The Whole Person Approach to Fitness

with Katharine Jones
Body and Soul

BEATING AGGRESSION

A Practical Guide for Working Women

Diana Lamplugh

WEIDENFELD AND NICOLSON · LONDON

First published in Great Britain in 1988 by
George Weidenfeld & Nicolson Limited,
91 Clapham High Street, London SW4 7TA

Copyright © 1988 by Diana Lamplugh

All rights reserved. No part of this publication may
be reproduced, stored in a retrieval system, or transmitted
in any form or by any means, electronic,
mechanical, photocopying, recording or otherwise,
without the prior permission of the copyright owner.

Photoset by Deltatype Ltd, Ellesmere Port
Printed by The Bath Press, Avon

On 28th July 1986
SUZY LAMPLUGH
was abducted while at work
without trace

She was 25 years old

'Though absent her light still shines'

This book is dedicated to my darling
daughter Suzy, and also to my other
children, Richard, Tami and Lizzie,
who are just as precious.

Diana Lamplugh 1987

The Suzy Lamplugh Trust

This Trust was founded on 4 December 1986 after the complete disappearance of Suzy Lamplugh, following a Monday-morning client appointment. The Suzy Lamplugh Trust aims to promote awareness and self-protection at work with particular focus on women; to encourage practical research, education and training to reduce personal vulnerability; to teach awareness, confidence and self-protection; to identify potential danger areas and to suggest practical ways of meeting them. The Trust needs money to fund active research into new aspects of vulnerability and for training schemes and packs to be used at places of work and at colleges and schools. All the royalties arising from the publication of this book will go to the Trust Funds.

Acknowledgements

I am wholly indebted to the excellent consultants who have helped me put this book together:

Sue Best	Inspector, Metropolitan Police Crime Prevention Unit
Tony Black	Clinical Psychologist/Mental Health Act Commissioner
Meg Bond	Assistant Director, Human Potential Research Project, Department of Educational Studies, University of Surrey
Mary-Helen Dewar	Stress Management Therapist, J.P.
Elizabeth Golder	Health Visitors Co-ordinator (Retired)
Professor Brian Groombridge	Director, Extra-Mural Studies, London University

Stevie Holland	Director, Managing Care Programme, South Bank Polytechnic
Lynne Howells	Training Consultant, Women's Unit, Birmingham City Council
Andy McDermott	Kent County Council
Paul Slaughter	Paladin Security
Marcia Reynolds	Management consultant
Margot Waddell	The Tavistock Clinic
Ray Wyre	Counsellor and authority on rape and male sex offenders
Dr Helen Zarod	Assertiveness Trainer

As you will see from the Contents, some of these consultants contributed a great deal of the work on which this book has been based. They are all experts in their own fields with many years' experience. They have put in many hours of dedicated work on behalf of the Trust and we are all indebted to them.

I would also like to thank Elaine Bishop, the Trust Administrator, for working out the computer and then spending hour upon hour typing, retyping and then doing it again – and again.

Lastly, I cannot forget to thank my husband, Paul, who has encouraged me, fed me and looked after the house while continuing his own work. Without his support the stress level might have been much higher! We make a good partnership.

Contents

Frontispiece

'On the Qui Vive'

When I had finished the first draft of this book I bravely sent it away to the Trust Consultants and secretly dreaded the return of all the manuscripts scored in red. In the event their marks were of course invaluable and I spent hours changing and editing to get it right. However, it was probably Brian Groombridge who focused my attention. He is the Professor of Adult Education and Director of the Extra-Mural Department of London University. His strength is his vision – he has an amazing conceptual overview which enables me to see a project in perspective. Brian said I had to answer three questions:

- What is this book about?
- What is it not about?
- And who is it for?

He made me think and I decided that this was vital information for any prospective buyer and deserved answering right at the beginning.

What is this book about?

Well, it teaches you about life skills which can help you work more effectively and efficiently, with awareness and without fear. I started out to write a book giving women a variety of methods of self-protection against aggression found in and around the workplace; however, it gradually became more than that, and it is now a book which gives strategies, techniques and skills with which you can learn to live life more fully, knowing yourself and your own personal way ahead.

What is this book not about?

This book is not directly concerned with the wider issues of aggression. I have left uncovered several areas which need to be faced with urgency by society as a whole; violence or aggression, whichever term you use, is an unpleasant, fearful aspect of our culture which must be tackled from many angles – environmental, political, racial and financial, taking into account gender, class, disability and problems such as alcohol and drugs. You will, I know, find many strategies which are totally valid and urgently required but which are not catered for in this book. Here I have concentrated primarily on the individual.

Who is this book for?

This book is for all working women, whoever you are and in whatever capacity you work. It is also concerned with the individual woman as a citizen, a colleague, an executive or manager, and in these roles as one individual combining with another and yet another to become formidable pressure groups. These groups can and will ensure discussion, action and change. I hope this book is for you.

Why have I written this book?

While writing this book I began to realize that it was also about my own search for a fuller life through the help of many experts in varied fields. This has come about not as a defence measure against aggression and my daughter Suzy's disappearance, but as a positive reaction to my daughter's love of living and my desire to enable others to be on the 'qui vive', which is usually translated as 'alertness' but which means literally 'who lives?'. Suzy has left me with a mission in life. Our Trust motto comes from T.S. Eliot, and hopes that 'From the end is the beginning.' If this book helps you and other working women, then Suzy's life will not have been in vain.

Diana Lamplugh
October 1987

Introduction

I wanted to call this book *Lines and Squares* because I remember a chubby little girl sent off round a Cheltenham square to her first school. It seemed a long way and it often felt lonely, and, as I recall it, I was not that keen to arrive, so I played two games. One was that if I touched all the railings without exception I would have good luck, but the railings were disappearing bit by bit; they were hauled off to add to the war effort. The other, more enduring game was the one I had learned from A. A. Milne. Keep to the pavement squares and all was well, step on the lines and the bears appeared. Somehow, I think the precautions I will give you in this book to help you protect yourself from aggression in the workplace are similar to 'treading on the squares' – straightforward and simple, but requiring diligence and application. No one need invite the bears!

When the publishers suggested the more direct and briefer title *Beating Aggression*, I hesitated. At first sight, 'beating' seemed an aggressive word in itself. However, I looked it up and other meanings were: to defeat or subdue; to excel or surpass; to evade or overcome; to succeed or forestall; to make or count time; to perplex or baffle; to progress against; to force to retreat or withdraw. Seen in this light the word could hardly be more appropriate and I was delighted to agree.

Many of you are mothers, aunts, sisters, certainly friends – but all of us are daughters, so I am sure that you must have an inkling of the horror my husband and I felt when the unthinkable happened to us. Our lovely sparkling daughter was abducted without trace on Monday, 28 July 1986, in the course of her job as an estate agent.

Suzy could have been you or someone in your family – she was happy, loved, full of fun – a girl who enjoyed her life and her job. She made every effort to keep fit and healthy, excelling in sports such as tennis, swimming and windsurfing. She had travelled the path one always hoped for one's daughter, enjoying school and working hard, singing in the church choir, becoming a Queen's Guide, training to become a beautician, working her way round the world on the *QE2*, making her own clothes, buying her own car, settling down, doing up her own flat, and establishing herself with a group of like-minded energetic friends whose 'high' was outdoor exercise, not drugs. At twenty-five Suzy was fulfilled, but also on the threshold of a useful and exciting life.

Like many young women today, Suzy was extremely confident in her work and abilities; in all ways she felt equal to her male colleagues. In her work she was unaware of and uninterested in any difference between the sexes. When Suzy made that routine call one Monday lunchtime, acting purely in her role as negotiator for a firm of estate agents, it seems she was off-guard and did not sense her vulnerability. An awareness of potential danger, a healthy respect for the male, his actions and reactions, might have helped to prevent her falling into an obvious trap.

It cannot be stressed too strongly that the problems I am concerned with here are society's problems, not just women's problems. It is often difficult for women to be taken seriously by men. Men need to start taking responsibility for their own behaviour and that of other members of their sex.

Suzy's abduction has brought to the surface a realization of the often ignored hazards and dangers faced by the increasingly adventurous, ambitious and skilled women setting out with determination to conquer new fields in today's world. In my experience, women want to be able to work on an equal basis with their male colleagues, but to do so they need to be equipped with awareness and a knowledge of how to thrive.

We set up the Suzy Lamplugh Trust in the hope that we can fill this gap. We have been busy ever since its launch in December 1986 raising public awareness, publishing our magazine, *The Acorn* (from little acorns mighty oaks do grow); producing our first video, *Avoiding Danger*, with the National Association of Citizens Advice Bureaux; instigating conferences and seminars and giving talks to organizations as diverse as the BMA and the Farmers' Union, universities and the Soroptimists. It was in a meeting resulting from one of these talks that this book was commissioned.

My main concern has been to encourage courses which will, I hope, become an integral part of the training programmes of most organizations. Employees and employers, men and women, should be working together to share problems, raise awareness, gain skills and identify changes. I hope that organizations will foster more mutual confidence between staff and managers, so that they will be able to assess the problem of aggression together and discuss designing or redesigning a strategy for preventive measures. I hope that this will be followed up by the implementation of the strategy with continued support, sympathetic consideration and increased respect between employers and employees. It is because I believe that everyone in the workplace needs to know and understand the problems that I think it is imperative that these courses be for both men and women of whatever status, working together towards a common goal.

However, I began to realize that it was not enough for the Suzy Lamplugh Trust to set its sights solely on employers setting up courses with enthusiasm across the board. Despite the fact that feedback on existing courses has emphasized their benefits (employees now know how to cope with situations and, if necessary, how to defend themselves; they are more assertive in dealing not only with the public but also with their colleagues; and there has been a positive effect on staff motivation and job satisfaction), it is unlikely that all employers will immediately see the benefit to their organizations. Many of them will still be concerned that such courses may serve as a deterrent to women workers, heightening their fear. For this reason it is vital that all the information and knowledge should be immediately available to the individual, and in particular to women.

My aim in this book is to motivate and enable you, the working woman, wherever you work and whoever you work for, even if you are self-employed or a manager, to be better equipped to protect yourself and to avoid, defuse or cope with aggression in its many forms. Of course I agree that women should not be asked to shoulder the blame and burden of this self-protection on their own. It is imperative to create more understanding and change the attitudes and behaviour of aggressors. However, I think that is going to be a long-term enterprise. We have now within our reach well-researched and easily attainable methods we can use. There seems no reason why we cannot help ourselves.

What is the problem?

Despite headlines such as 'Rapist Attacked Jail Visitor', 'When Terror Is A Factor Of Life' ('The issue of violence has never been more talked about in social work circles, reactions vary from outrage to resignation'); 'Attacking The Problem Of Violence Against GPs' ('Will more publicity stem the tide of violence against GPs or increase it further? asks . . .'), and so on, I still get asked if I am not being emotive and whether I am just exaggerating a minor problem. I would like you to consider that, on the contrary, we have only recently discovered the tip of an iceberg.

Consider these responses from a recent study by Holden (1985) of the nursing profession:

'There is a widespread acceptance of aggressive behaviour towards nurses – we are seen as easy targets.'

'Nursing staff are made to feel it is their own fault when assaulted (verbally or otherwise) and to turn the other cheek. Everybody considers the patient but not the nurse.'

'Verbal attacks can be just as stressful as physical attacks. We do not believe there is enough care and support of nursing staff by other professionals when nurses are exposed to aggressive behaviour.'

It was noted that after an attack nurses felt abused and emotionally exploited. They wanted to provide high-quality care, but they felt angry and resentful. They wanted to help yet they felt helpless; in fact they wanted to nurture the very patients by whom they were made anxious and afraid. Some respondents captured this dilemma with the following statements:

'What more can you add – we live in an aggressive, selfish society.'

'I have been subjected to verbal abuse on almost every shift I work. It is part and parcel of the job.'

'These questions assume that these aggressive incidents are fairly isolated – usually they happen on an almost daily basis.'

This is a health visitor's story:

'I called on a family who had an elderly man living in the same house. He was an uncle who had been sent home from America by a daughter who could not cope. The man was on his own and invited me into the kitchen where he was making tea. I felt uneasy – intuitively I wanted to leave but didn't. I thought, this is ridiculous, he is an eighty-five-year-old man and I have to do this visit. In the kitchen he grabbed me and tried to strangle me – after what seemed hours but was probably seconds I broke loose and ran out the back door, climbing over a fence. I landed on top of a surprised neighbour who gave me a lift home. I left my diary and bag in the house and these were later returned by the family. My manager's response was to reprimand me for leaving a diary in a patient's home! The potential danger of the incident was ignored. No note was put on the record for future staff. I learnt some good lessons: (a) go with your instincts – if you feel unsafe get out or get help; (b) do not assume that because a client is old or handicapped he or she is less dangerous; (c) record the incident in order that other staff can be protected; (d) inform other professionals such as social workers, district nurses and GPs. It may not happen to them but at least they should be warned.'

A survey conducted in 1987 by the World Travel Agency found Britain one of the worst places in the world for women to get good hotel service. Responses from 180 female executives showed that women had little chance of drinking alone in a hotel bar without harassment. [*The Times*, 3 September 1987]

One in three GPs have been the victims of threatened or actual violence or verbal abuse, according to a major study on violence in the health service published yesterday. The commonest problem is verbal abuse, suffered by a quarter of all GPs. A further 5 per cent have been threatened with weapons and 1 per cent actually assaulted, half of them seriously. [*The General Practitioner*, 8 May 1987]

Lynne Howells, of the Women's Unit at Birmingham City Council, writes:

'For staff, within the public and private sector, dealing with members of the public face to face can often feel like a difficult and thankless task. The complexities of dealing with a changing public are often underestimated and little thought is given to the training and support staff need to carry out their work efficiently at the same time as providing for the consumers a caring service.'

Public sector

Within the public sector there is increasing difficulty in providing adequate services to meet the expressed need of the public at large. Tensions can occur as the front-line staff bear immediate responsibility for explaining to the consumer cutbacks, policies and procedures over which they have had little control. The commitment of staff to a consumer-centred approach will often depend on their own feelings of satisfaction and security, which themselves will depend to some extent on staffing levels, hours of work, level of managerial support, and other working conditions. In turn consumers can easily feel uncared for and frustrated by what they experience as unhelpful bureaucratic systems and procedures.

AGGRESSION AND VIOLENCE

Being on the front line means being increasingly aware of situations which are potentially violent. For staff the fear of dealing with a range of difficult situations is increasing. When the Royal College of Nursing sent out a questionnaire, 68 per cent of nurses claimed they had either been threatened or assaulted. It was found that nurses experiencing potentially violent situations over a period of time became ill and often simply left the service.

Social workers are another key group whose ability to carry out their jobs effectively is hampered by their fear of violence. There is a reality in these fears. Frances Bettridge, a social worker from Solihull, was killed in September 1986 in the home of one of her clients, who was also killed by her common-law husband. Surveys have shown that on average each social worker can expect to be attacked once a year. Birmingham City Council have recently passed a policy agreeing that staff should be trained in dealing with aggression, giving priority to women and those working in situations of greatest risk. Other councils and health authorities are formulating similar policies.

UNIONS

Unions, obviously, are concerned about this problem. Following the death of Carolyn Puckett in 1986, the Health Visitors' Association issued guidelines to its members and began to run training courses on dealing with aggression. NALGO and COHSE have also issued guidelines in an attempt to deal with the problem realistically.

Private sector

It is not only the public sector with its shrinking resources where tensions occur. The disappearance of Suzy has caused other agencies dealing with the public to reassess the need for training and for organizational change to create a safer working environment for their employees.

The need for a realistic approach

Most approaches to dealing with aggression and violence at work look broadly at the factors which aggravate potentially aggressive situations, in order to provide staff with skills to defuse those situations. This is important but it fails in one significant respect.

The majority of public-sector employees, including those in the NHS, are women (over 60 per cent). Women experience and respond to potentially violent situations in a very particular way. It is essential to recognize that the way women handle difficult situations is often dominated by the real fear for their own safety, and that aggression towards women workers occurs in the wider context of increasing violence towards all women.

This book is dedicated to all working women . . .

Looking back I am horrified by the risks I took and the hazards I faced during my own life as a young girl going out to work. I have to admit that I would not have been so lucky today. Even so, I had some tough lessons to face. In my first job as a receptionist/secretary in a telecommunications base I became the butt of much sexual harassment from the drivers. I gather I 'put them in their place' by a look of distaste but it also earned me the nickname of 'Toffeenose', which hurt. At my second job, as a headmaster's secretary, I became the target of a matron who suggested that I led on the boys and masters with my glances and clothes. I ended up nearly leaving the job. It is only in retrospect that I recognize this as verbal abuse prompted by jealousy. At the time I felt perplexed and diminished.

My next job took me round the country as secretary to the owner of an opera company. We travelled to a new town each week or fortnight by our own train. Arriving on a Sunday, we toured the streets looking for digs, searching for bedbugs with pieces of soap and locking our doors to ensure the landlord or oboe player left us alone. Despite seeing a woman having her face slashed in Liverpool, where we had been advised to go around in pairs, I still walked down Sauchiehall Street in Glasgow at midnight after the show in a white dress. There was a heatwave and I enjoyed the freedom, casually turning down the kerb crawlers and stepping over the drunks. I must have been mad, but I wonder now that I had so little fear or caution. I survived a rape attempt in Hull because I had my period and calmly enquired if he minded being splashed all over with blood. He disappeared without trace. He was a friend of a friend who felt that anyone in the theatre was 'on the game' – I think both of us were horrified, but of course that was over thirty-odd years ago.

Now I come to think of it, my experiences did nothing to make me take self-protection in the workplace with any seriousness at all. I gave Suzy no warning, nor help or thoughts on precautions she should take. I cannot leave *you* like that, especially now I have learned that there is so much help available. It will not be easy to remember or to put into action, but it will be more than worthwhile. I suggest that you read the book through to get the general picture and then start again, taking it stage by stage. Learn the bits that most apply to you and keep dipping into the other sections.

I began to sift the wheat from the chaff. In the first place I began to realize that many of us can actually invite aggression by our own attitudes and tension. Tension control helps all aspects of our lives. The technique is very much part of the Slimnastics programme, and the classes which I teach in relaxation. It is also very much part of my own way of living, so I feel more qualified in this respect. Some of the attitudes in the second chapter may seem like common sense but some are so straightforward that they are often forgotten. In both these chapters I have had much help from Meg Bond, of the University of Surrey Human Potential Research Project, and Stevie Holland, at the South Bank Polytechnic. Meg and Stevie are gifted teachers and from them I have learned a great deal. I hope you will learn alongside me.

Assertiveness and Transactional Analysis are completely new skills for me. When I am giving talks I often ask how many of the audience have ever attended Assertiveness or Transactional Analysis courses. I never cease to be amazed by the lack of hands which are raised. I realize that the two phrases have earned themselves a reputation for being contrived and fairly cranky (assertion becomes confused with aggression itself, especially as far as women are concerned), but I have discovered that both are merely techniques for better communications and are very useful. These two skills can create a better atmosphere both in and out of the workplace, and it is hard to understand why all women, in this enlightened age, are not encouraged to develop them. I would go so far as to say that they should be part of the sixth-form curriculum in schools. Marcia Reynolds, a leading authority in TA and now a management consultant, was my tutor in this technique. Meg Bond, with a team from South Bank Polytechnic, designed the Assertiveness course which I will work through with you. I hope you benefit as much as I have. I also envisage you having as much fun trying out the technique as I did. I had great trouble not boring friends by grabbing them to boast how I had just made 'so-and-so' work.

Many women go out of their way to avoid violence. But, I reasoned, many of them were going to have to face it if they intended to go on working well in their chosen jobs. It was a relief to me to find out that there are many simple measures, given in the Avoidance section, which will allow you a freer life with more access to work potential. Many women work at or from home too, so I have ensured that safety there is covered as well.

In this section I have been supported and helped by the Metropolitan Police, especially by Inspector Sue Best of the Crime Prevention Unit. We have had many gripes from the women's movement and others about the attitudes of the police towards women. While many of them still ring true, the Force is conscious of the need for change. I believe that it is much better to work with the Establishment, urging them to consider attitudes and improve techniques, rather than against them. So far I have been impressed by the way they are pushing aside the old image of locks and bolts and working towards methods of self-protection which are applicable to the way women live their lives today.

I have Stevie Holland and Tony Black to thank for the massive research which went into the Aggression chapter. I found their thoughts and ideas very helpful and again could not understand why they were not widely known. Ray Wyre is the leading authority on rape in Great Britain, and he has worked a great deal in the USA. His thoughts are new, thought-provoking, but I feel invaluable. They have given me a new insight and a more cautious view of some male approaches. The final conclusion is probably the most important in that it gives you many ideas which can be actively implemented within your workplace and that is why I have entitled it 'Action'. In this section I have benefited from the excellent work which Lynne Howells has been doing with Birmingham County Council.

All this is very authoritative stuff, but I hope you will also find it readable and easy to put into practice. I have written it in the only way I can – as a non-expert but as a working woman wanting to know how best to protect myself. Having now worked my way through all this material – the exercises, the ideas, the research and the recommend-ations – I feel more of an expert, and confident enough to have no doubt that many women will find this book just what they discover they have needed all along.

I am sitting here today in the room which used to belong to Suzy. I am remembering the hard work she put into painting it and making it 'all hers'. It seems a long time ago but on the other hand it seems only yesterday. Now it is my study and I love it – it is very conducive to work and amazingly peaceful.

The summer of 1986 was to be the beginning of our year of renovation. Three of our children had moved away ages before and we had decided to increase our mortgage and do everything to the house, while we were both still working, which would give us pleasure as we grew older. The builders came the very day Suzy disappeared – 'Not before time!' she had said when we told her that at last our plans were coming to fruition.

The last time we saw Suzy was that Sunday evening before she disappeared. We were waiting for the builders to move in. I had been hard at work removing her paintwork and the many layers of paper underneath. I persuaded her to come and look at my handiwork and my choice of decorations. 'It's super, Mum,' she said, 'but the paper is ghastly – you can't possibly have it!' I went paranoid about that paper after Suzy disappeared. 'I'll have to get another – I'll have to change it . . .' 'Do you like it?' asked a psychiatrist friend. 'Of course,' I answered. 'Well, stand up for yourself,' he said. I took his advice, the paper was hung and it looks lovely. I now think and hope Suzy might approve of it too.

I learned a valuable lesson over that wallpaper. We all have to make our own decisions. I was amazed that I could have the confidence to think for myself under such terrible circumstances. We all have that ability, but it is essential that we gain the courage to foster it. If we do and we are faced by aggression either in or out of the workplace, we might surprise ourselves with our ability to cope.

Suzy was a lovely person; when she was happy and excited she 'glowed' – people truthfully described her as 'lighting up a room'. We miss her appallingly. There is and always will be a huge gap in our lives and an ache in our hearts. But although she is not with us now her light will shine on. Out of a truly horrible situation there will be a positive outcome if enough women take up the challenge to protect themselves and persuade their employers that it is a vital element of working life. Suzy will live on through the Trust in her name.

I cannot take credit for being the sole author of this book. I see myself more as a catalyst. Because of my work as co-founder of the British Slimnastics Association I have not only written the books but also been much involved in the manuals for the leaders and their tutors. I have personally suffered through taking and attaining the new Certificate of Adult and Further Education. This has all taught me to value learning, teaching and logical thought. It was these values I brought to bear on the wealth of ideas and material which was presented to me from many sources as being valid and necessary in learning to deal with aggression.

Diana Lamplugh
October 1987

CHAPTER 1

Stress and tension control

Consultants:

STEVIE HOLLAND
Polytechnic of the South Bank

MEG BOND
Assistant Director, Human Potential
Research Project, University of Surrey

All passages denoted by marginal arrows are directly derived from
Stevie Holland, 'Stress in Nursing', Workbook and Reader for the
Distance Learning Centre, Polytechnic of the South Bank, London,
1987, except where otherwise indicated; and except for the section
on 'Night work' (pp. 28–29) which is directly derived from David
Minors, James Waterhouse and Simon Folkard, 'Out of Rhythm',
Nursing Times, 10 April 1985; and the section on 'Coping
mechanisms' (pp. 33–37) which is directly derived from Meg Bond,
Stress and Self-Awareness: A Guide for Nurses, Heinemann, London,
1986.

When I began to receive and collect material for this book, I noticed one common denominator running through all the sections: this was the need to fully understand the strains and stresses of the workplace and to learn relaxation techniques to cope with them. Tension control appears to be a neglected area; it features very rarely in any awareness, self-protection or self-defence programme. The effects of stress and tension on both physical and mental health are well known and documented; so is their relationship with work performance and attendance. However, the link between tension and aggression is often overlooked.

There are many reasons why we are affected by tension: we may be tired, unfit, insecure, unhappy, threatened or afraid. All these conditions can lower our tolerance level and make us prone to the aggression of others. We need to recognize our own stresses and practise the skills of relaxation, especially when we are actually in vulnerable situations.

Aggression can breed aggression. Even when talking with a friend, if either of you takes a hostile stance both of you are likely to feel stressed and tense. You may react by either meeting it head on or by cringing with averted eyes; both reactions are likely to raise the aggression level still further. If this happens with a stranger, client, customer or colleague, the results could be most unfortunate for you and your work. Interpersonal communication can be much easier when you have mastered tension control.

In a really dangerous situation, too, you can be frozen to the spot by tension, unable to utter a sound. All those muscles will need to be released before you can scream and run. Tension control and relaxation underpin all the other techniques in this book. With these acquired skills you can think and act with greater confidence and precision. It seems a good point at which to start beating aggression.

This is a topic on which I feel able to speak entirely for myself, without any reference to other experts. But I have not allowed my feelings to overrule my head; I have consulted with Meg Bond, of the University of Surrey Human Potential Research Centre, and Stevie Holland, of the South Bank Polytechnic. Their work, especially in relating stress and tension to the workplace, has been invaluable.

My own understanding of stress and tension has developed over a period of at least twenty years. Long ago when I was still comparatively innocent, I began to see the relationship between overweight and overstress. As this was relevant to our work in designing programmes for Slimnastics, I began to research ways in which we could use our classes to help students cope with stress and tension.

I decided to attend a course run under the University of London Extra-Mural Department by Joe Macdonald Wallace, who is now European Director of the International Stress and Tension Control Society UK. These classes, which were then called 'Neuromuscular Relaxation', were aimed at those in the teaching profession. I went along to learn to teach, and at the end of the course I came away a completely different person!

With four children, a growing organization to run and books to write, I felt I had a busy life, but also a fulfilled and happy one. I had no idea how much I was suffering both physically and mentally from tension. I used to have what I called 'sinus headaches' – after I learned to put Joe's techniques into practice they completely disappeared; I used to think I was constantly sitting in draughts, especially when driving, as I often had appalling pains up the back of the neck which spread right up the back of my head (which I never connected with stress and the tension involved in driving), but they too have gone. Previously, I had relied on the pills prescribed by my doctor or had resorted to my own prescription of aspirin or an alcoholic drink to get temporary relief. Now I do not need them.

There was an added bonus as well. I not only suffered less, I was also able to think better, especially under stressful conditions. Progressive Relaxation works on the principle that whereas tension in the muscles provokes an 'alert' response in the brain which floods the body with all the aids for dealing actively with a stressful situation, reversing the process by releasing the tension and relaxing the muscles will cancel the panic signals to and from the brain. All the energy can then be directed to cope with the problem in hand. This means that the natural reaction to stress – tension – can through knowledge and practice be controlled. I have tried it out in many situations and every time I have been amazed at how well it has helped me to keep cool and in control of myself, and even sometimes to enjoy or perhaps just make the most of times which would previously have tied me in knots.

I was, in my own estimation, asked to withstand the ultimate stress for a mother – the complete disappearance of her daughter under mysterious and inexplicable circumstances, and with horrible criminal implications. The stress and resulting tension has dragged on for many months and through many additional traumas. It is one thing which I would have had no doubt would 'break' me completely, had someone suggested it before it happened. Indeed, I shied away in horror when any friend or even acquaintance lost a child; I was traumatized into silence and the resulting guilt made it impossible for me to express to them my feelings and condolences. I was able to identify completely with those who were affected similarly by our situation. I really feel that without the skills I had been taught and the constant practice of the techniques of tension control I would have been unable to survive as I have.

However, ours are exceptional circumstances. Here we are thinking more particularly with reference to women in the workplace. Learning and practising tension control techniques needs some dedication, time and effort, so I want to convince you that it is relevant and worthwhile. First of all, you must know more about the stress which causes tension.

Hans Selye, the father of stress control and the mentor of Joe Macdonald Wallace, wrote: 'Stress is an underlying response of the body – complete freedom from stress is death.' Everyone experiences stress; it is part of the driving force by which we achieve our goals. However there is an optimum level of stress compatible with our health, both mental and physical. Understimulation or overstimulation may both lead to 'distress'. One more quote from Selye will put this in perspective: 'Stress cannot be avoided. The art is to learn how to live a full life with a minimum amount of wear and tear. The secret is . . . to live more intelligently.'

1 Tension and anger

If we think of those occasions when we have been truly afraid or very angry, we can remember some of the more obvious physical symptoms of stress – taut muscles, clenched teeth, pounding heart, rapid breathing, sweating palms, dry mouth. It can work the other way too. Stress – or rather overstress – can result in aggression. The following story appeared first in a book I wrote with Pamela Nottidge called *Stress and Overstress* (now published as the *Commonsense Guide to Stress Control*, Slimnastics Books). The account is probably the more effective as I wrote it only a few years after the incident:

One overstressed day I particularly remember. I then had three children under four, and I think it must have been during a holiday because they were all at home, no playschool for the eldest. It was also pretty foul weather, and the youngest was snivelling with a cold, the three-year-old was proving hard to potty-train and the middle one was having temper tantrums (real humdingers when she beat her head against the doors).

Despite being the eldest of four myself, I never had to look after children, as my mother always had help and I was certainly not a natural homemaker, mother, nursemaid, seamstress or cleaner. I loathed the endless round of housework and would much rather have been back at my job in the BBC. I loved my children dearly but hated the monotonous and claustrophobic round of scraps and falls, cut knees and sobs, washing and ironing, tidying and cleaning, fish fingers or sausages, instant whips and biscuits.

The day I am recalling was worse than most, as the cold and the rain prevented even a welcome walk in the nearby park. Keeping my patience through the crawling hours of the day was a major task and I decided to do some cooking to relieve the tedium. I chose home-made onion soup as the ingredients were to hand and I had been unable to go out shopping.

Giving myself this fling did not go unimpeded. The dog was sick, the babies piddled in their pants, drew on the walls, broke a teapot and squabbled. Bath time and bed were a relief to all. After one final quarrel which resulted in the middle one crying herself to sleep, I scrambled round the house to tidy up before the breadwinner's return. He was late! I longed for him to come home; I had not talked to anyone over five during the whole day, except the milkman, and even he had been surly. Anyway, what was my man up to living in his fascinating free world full of trains and people, business lunches, uninterrupted spells of thought and writing, and contact with the opposite sex? What *was* he up to?!

Now I was worried. I knew I looked a frump, had little conversation except the children's teeth and was fretful and nagging. The minutes ticked by. At last I heard the key in the door. I never noticed his tired face or realized that he was worried about his job. As he slipped on a tiny car with one wheel missing that had somehow escaped my notice I heard him swear under his breath about 'toys all over the place'; my anger was rising. At last when he eventually sat down for the evening meal he stared down at the soup and exclaimed (with some justification), 'This is horribly greasy.'

I picked up the soup plate and smashed it over his head. I loved him with all my heart but I had slaved over that soup! Luckily, he was not scalded and forgave me, but he had a nasty cut on his head.

That small scar always serves as a reminder of how, for one moment, I was stressed beyond all reason. My aggression was the result of how I was feeling. It is seldom any one factor which makes people act in this way. As a result of a combination of under- and over-stimulation – a series of small incidents building up emotions of anger and frustration combined with hopes, fears and expectations which failed to material-ize – I acted in a way which was both dangerous and, I hope, out of character.

Could this happen in the workplace? Well, consider this scenario given to me by Stevie Holland:

> You set the alarm for 6.30 – it fails to go off – you wake at 7.15 – dash out of bed, stub your toe on the dressing table – throw on some clothes – do not have time for breakfast. It's snowing outside – you have to take time to clean the windscreen but you don't have time to do it properly and can hardly see to drive. Although the car starts, it keeps cutting out and you are getting more anxious that it may break down. At the gates of your work a man steps out in front of you and you nearly skid into a wall in order to avoid him. You blast your horn in anger. By the time you reach the office you are late, cold, hungry, angry and in no mood for any more hassle. The office manager looks up and says, 'Why are you late? This just won't do. I'll have to report you.'

Does this sound familiar? We have all had this kind of day, when a series of events makes us very stressed. It is often these repeated incidences of stress which we may fail to deal with that make us likely to be aggressive.

When we talk about harmful stress we usually mean emotional stress. Often called arousal, it comes in many guises and its causes are not always unpleasant. Fear and anger generate stress, but so does the pulse-quickening excitement of an adventure, a sport or falling in love. Some people seem to thrive on stress, drawing on its stimulus for their peak performance, or enjoying being 'kept on their toes'. Yet for others it can be totally destructive. Stress is said to be one of the major causes of human breakdown at work, what is called 'job burnout'.

Our reaction to stress is a primitive one, handed down to us by our stone-age ancestors. For them it was a vital response to danger. Known as the fright/fight/flight response, it was in the days of primitive humans precisely that – the marshalling of all the body's resources to fight danger and win or to run away and escape. Only those with the fastest and most dynamic response survived. So, by natural selection, twentieth-century humans are descended from a long line of highly successful ancestors with superb reactions to stress situations.

Tension control can therefore be seen as a vital ingredient of a successful career. Dynamic response combined with control must be an asset for those who wish to get ahead. It can also help to defuse aggression in yourself as well as others. I experienced a very acute illustration of this during one of the 'dramatic' phases in the police hunt for my daughter's abductor. I find it very difficult to operate if I am kept in the dark by the police and have to rely on reports from the media which often vary wildly. On this occasion, the top brass called me to headquarters. By this time, I was not only very worried, I was also extremely angry. For once, I neglected to defuse my aggression by actively employing my tension control technique. The resultant conversation turned into a slanging match which led nowhere constructive. Luckily, once I had blown my top, I recognized my mistake and gradually, as I gained control over my tension, I defused my own aggression and this lessened their defensive reaction until we together achieved an even keel. Once there, we were able to make some positive progress which was a relief to us all.

2 Stress and your body

Without some tension in your body you would be unable to breathe, think, see, speak, keep upright, be lively or alert. Your muscles need some 'tone' to support your skeleton; you also need the stimulation of the brain and hormones to help you to see, think, talk, react and anticipate. Some tension is good for you in order to heighten your feelings and enjoyment of life.

It is, however, when stress causes constant or excessive tension, or when stress is too much to stand and the emotional reaction is intense or prolonged, that tension can be the cause not only of behavioural problems such as aggression but can also result in actual physical harm. At the very least it may interfere with your performance or your happiness. Learning to control such tension is a life-enhancing skill.

Attempts have been made to relate the likelihood of a heart attack to a personality type. Researchers have divided male subjects into two groups: Type A and Type B. Type A have a chronic sense of time-urgency, are aggressive, ambitious, and may drive themselves on to meet deadlines (often self-imposed). They are self-demanding, often doing two or three things at once, impatient and always in a hurry. They are likely to react with hostility to anything that seems to get in their way and are temperamentally incapable of letting up. They are also likely to think they are indispensable. This adds up to a state of constant stress. Type B men exhibit the opposite characteristics: they are less competitive, less preoccupied with achievement, less rushed and generally more easygoing, not allowing their lives to be governed by deadlines. They are better at separating work from play and they know how to relax. They are less prone to anger, and do not feel constantly impatient, rushed and under pressure. The incidence of heart attacks is much higher in Type A than in Type B individuals.

However, most people are a mixture of both A and B, or may exhibit the characteristics of either according to the occasion, and in some the real mix of A and B might not be immediately apparent. It is also quite possible, as you will see from the physiological responses to stress discussed below, for a biochemical reaction to occur even though there has been no bodily sign of tension. The human body is a very complex and, in many areas, still undiscovered or imperfectly understood territory. You may not feel in need of tension control, you may feel completely relaxed, or you may think that you have not got the time to waste. Do not let yourself be fooled. Everyone can benefit from learning the Tension Control Technique (TCT). It will stand you in good stead all your life.

3 Tension and your body

The 'red alert' response

Watch a rabbit in a field when it senses a 'presence' – it sits up, the ears stretch high, the nose twitches and the eyes are bright as, frozen for a moment, it assesses the situation. If it's another male impinging on already marked territory, the rabbit springs forward to thump the ground and see off the enemy; if it's a human, the rabbit shows its white bobtail and back feet as a warning to the others before disappearing down the burrow. Occasionally it's a false alarm, but, to make sure, the rabbit drops down and becomes motionless until once more it can relax and carry on eating.

Think of your response when, walking home through a dark street, you suddenly become aware that someone might be following you:

your expression freezes, your ears feel almost as if they are stretching backwards as you locate the sounds. How near are they? Are they menacing? You might feel angry and turn to face the oncomer or more likely you would run away from the suspected danger; just occasionally you might be 'rooted to the spot' until you feel secure again. These responses are the natural and very necessary defences you need for self-preservation.

Your whole body is affected by this 'red alert' response; the sense organs, most frequently those of sight or hearing, receive the signal of alarm and pass it on to the brain where its significance is recognized and from which messages are sent along the nerves to the muscles and to other organs. The muscles contract, often very abruptly as in the startled response. If the state of alertness or arousal continues, muscle activity and tension remain high and enable you to be more capable of reacting quickly to any further alert.

The signal from the eyes and ears via the brain and on to the muscles, which in turn contract into tension, acts as a trigger for:

- *a changed heart rate* which is usually increased (most people know the feeling of the fast-beating heart after a near miss when driving). However, some people in anticipation of shock or unpleasantness feel their heart slowing down and beating forcibly.

- *a rise in blood pressure*, often to a very high level, which can remain for some time.

- *an effect on the blood vessels* throughout the body: those in the muscles open up so that more blood can course through them; those in the abdomen and in the skin contract so that less blood goes through them. The output of the heart is diverted from the skin and gut to the muscle of the trunk and limbs in preparation for greater muscular effort. As a direct cause of this, you become very pale and the stomach becomes flabby, giving you a heavy 'sinking' feeling.

- *an increase in sweating* in fairly specific areas such as the skin around the mouth and nose, the temples, the armpits, between the legs and especially the palms of the hands and the soles of the feet. The nervous public speaker can literally stream with perspiration.

- *a drying up of the saliva* and an increase in the secretion of gastric acid: the gastro-intestinal tract is markedly affected although movements of the stomach may diminish. The intestines are more active and may churn and gurgle. You may feel an urge to open your bowels. The bladder is similarly affected and there is an urge to pass water as the bladder muscle increases its activity. We all recognize the need to visit the toilet before an interview or important meeting.

- *the dilation of the pupils* of your eyes, to let in more light and help them to function in a more sensitive manner. Your other senses are similarly affected.

- *an expansion of the breathing tubes* (bronchi) which allows more air to be drawn into the lungs.

- *a change in your hormones.* This is less immediate because its speed is determined by the rate of the blood's circulation round the body. Hormones are chemical substances which are secreted by glands, and which travel in the bloodstream to their particular sites of action. Many hormones are implicated in stress responses; the most important ones are adrenalin, noradrenalin, and cortisol or hydro-cortisone (an adrenocortical hormone). Different species of animal secrete adrenalin and noradrenalin in different proportions. In man adrenalin predominates, and when this and noradrenalin are secreted into the bloodstream they act on many organs and reinforce all the above effects. In addition, adrenalin influences the metabolic balance of the body, mobilizing energy reserves in the liver and in the muscles themselves, making glucose available for immediate energy demands.

You are now ready for ACTION!

The 'constant' tension response

But what happens if you are unable to respond with any 'action' when your body is fully prepared and ready? There you are, lying beneath the bedclothes convinced there is a burglar downstairs; your heart beats, your blood pressure rises, you grow pale, your pupils dilate, you breathe faster, feel butterflies in your stomach and your mouth is dry; you start to tremble and want to go to the loo, but you dare not move.

Similarly, day after day the boss or committee might thwart some plans which you have painstakingly worked out and considered and because of your less advanced position you have to accept their decision, clench your fists, grit your teeth and go back to the drawing board again.

Likewise, quarrelling, anxiety, decisions, deadlines and of course many other occasions leave you with your responses pent up and with no outlet. Your tension reactions have most likely set in motion all the 'red alert' responses, but because the appropriate response in each case *isn't* to run or fight and burn off the reaction, you are left instead with all the added chemicals flooding your body.

Everyone has an individual pattern of physiological and psychological response to an 'alert', and this pattern will tend to be repeated when another signal comes. This means that one person may show a marked increase in heartbeat while sweating only a little, while another may perspire profusely; one person may show a rise in blood pressure, another an increase in gastric acid or perhaps severe muscle tension. We develop our own particular physical reactions to these calls on our energies.

This results in our developing our own physical warning signals when tension has reached an uncontrollable level. You may recognize one or more of these physiological symptoms:

- throbbing head or headache
- grinding teeth, impacted nerve
- twitching eyes, tremulous voice
- pain spreading up the neck over the back of the head
- tightness in the throat, a feeling of choking
- overbreathing (hyperventilation)
- aches between the shoulderblades
- nail-biting, damaged cuticles, twiddling thumbs
- palpitations and chest discomfort
- skin rashes
- vomiting and indigestion
- diarrhoea and frequent urination
- backache in general, especially in the lower back
- tiredness, weakness, sweating, trembling, breathlessness, fainting or insomnia

Psychological symptoms can include:

- increase in smoking
- increase in alcohol intake
- a marked increase or decrease in appetite
- inability, or constant desire and ability, to sleep
- feelings of tiredness and exhaustion

- absent-mindedness, inefficiency, loss of interest, lack of concentration
- loss of sex drive
- feelings of inability to cope
- irritability, impulsiveness, loss of coordination
- depression

Feelings associated with stress include:

- worthlessness
- tiredness
- hopelessness
- guilt
- anxiety
- anger
- tension
- apprehension
- irritability
- depression

Many of these are also associated with aggression. The physiological symptoms are very similar.

There are many different ways in which people demonstrate their emotional reactions to stress. For instance, feelings of anxiety may be exhibited as either:

- insomnia or constant sleepiness
- seeking company or isolation
- lethargy or hyperactivity

All can be reactions to stress. Of course they may be symptoms of something else entirely, but if you have checked that you are not ill and you frequently experience one of these reactions, you should perhaps see your doctor. They are more probably warning signals that excess tension is making your body suffer. They may be unpleasant, but they are useful.

Your 'locked-in' response to tension and the corresponding physical reactions can contribute to actual bodily illness. Some illnesses are believed to be directly related, at least in part, to tension.

Professional burnout
Dr Desmond Kelly, one of the Patrons of the Suzy Lamplugh Trust, is the leading authority on this condition.

It is a progressive reaction, characterized by loss of idealism, energy and purpose. 'Burnout' is a relatively new term which is just entering the language in Britain, but it is very much part of the vocabulary in the United States and it has been researched there for some time. It was coined by a psychoanalyst, Dr Herbert Freudenberger (1974), who described it as a syndrome of 'physical and emotional exhaustion, involving the development of negative self-concepts, negative job attitudes and loss of concern and feeling for patients'.

There are four identifiable stages leading to burnout:

Stage 1   This may affect you especially when you are newly qualified or starting work, or when you have just moved to a new job location. You will have a feeling of uncertainty about coping with the demands of new pressures. Perhaps you will also have a great deal of enthusiasm and energy, with a tendency to be overconscientious and to overwork.

Stage 2   Now you may have shortlived bouts of irritation, tiredness, anxiety and frustration. There may be feelings of stagnation or 'beating your head against a brick wall', and a tendency to 'awfulize': 'Everything is awful!'

Stage 3   You probably feel increasing anger and resentment, lasting for longer periods. There will be feelings of failure and general discontent at work. Also increasing guilt, a lowering of self-esteem and feelings of inadequacy. Apathy will increase – you may feel 'Why bother?'

Stage 4   This is a state of extreme personal distress. It can be reflected by physical ailments such as ulcers, backache, headaches – all the physical symptoms we looked at earlier. It may lead to problems such as alcohol abuse and severe insomnia. There is a reluctance to go to work and feelings of complete failure and non-achievement.

The results of burnout are ultimately:

- job dissatisfaction
- sick leave
- reduced commitment to work
- distancing
- low morale

Although we have looked briefly at the burnout syndrome, it is a term which is really only correctly applied to a relatively small number of people. However, many of you will have experienced *some* of the symptoms of burnout, and will have witnessed it in your colleagues. If you feel worried about this, do seek help from your doctor.

4 Sources of stress at work

Before we can start to manage the negative work-related stress more effectively, by adjusting our coping strategies or by developing new ones, we need to find out what stress is. We are concentrating on stress issues at work, but obviously work and personal life impinge on each other; stress in one's personal life is equally important and needs to be treated just as sympathetically.

Of course there are many complex, often inter-related causes of stress and it is vital that you should examine your own perceptions of stress in your own working life. You need to consider:

- The nature of your work and your role within it
- Your interpersonal relationships
- The organizational context

THE NATURE OF YOUR WORK

Quantitative workload

Do you ever feel that you simply need more time to get through the tasks of each day? You may feel you have too little time to do what is expected of you (or what you expect of yourself) and you are often overwhelmed by conflicting priorities and will behave in an aggressive or defensive manner. To combat this you can deliberately try to improve your skill in decision-making. If you think clearly about the purpose and nature of problems, allowing sufficient time and consulting with others, it will improve the quality of your problem analysis. Then you can try to identify all possible solutions and consider likely repercussions. You can be decisive in selecting the most suitable solution and follow it through in application.

In order to manage your time better you need to undertake some frank self-appraisal about this aspect of your working life. The following points come from *How to Escape the Time Trap* by Ken Hyett. If you work in a team consider them together. Maybe you can work out a practical plan for improvement.

- *Priorities:* What are the priorities of your job? Does your allocation of time reflect these priorities? What are the most time-consuming activities?

- *Planning:* How far ahead can you plan your activities? How can planning be improved?
- *Control:* Are you able to stick to the plan? What are the causes of distraction? How can control of time be improved?
- *Delegation:* How effective is your delegation now? What tasks should/could be delegated to others?
- *Self-discipline:* How well organized are you in approaching your job? What improvements could be made – more punctual, more decisive, less accessible, less helpful, less time away from your desk?
- *Time traps:* How do you waste time in work at present? How can this time loss be reduced – preventing interruptions, fewer meetings, less social chat?
- *Management skills:* How effective are your skills in completing the main management tasks? What skills could be improved – faster reading or report-writing, more disciplined talking, running better meetings?

Physical demands

Many people at work have to face such physically strenuous demands that real strain and consequent pressure result; neck problems and bad backs can be the result of poorly sited machinery and furniture which is the wrong height. This can be made worse if it is accompanied by tension caused by stress. The long-term cumulative effects of stress can lead both to acute physical trauma and to chronic tiredness and the need to rest. Management need to be aware that more care in choosing equipment, alternating teams of workers and ensuring health checks would reduce stress-related days of absence.

Emotional demands

Most workers want to do a good job. Sometimes this can seem impossible because of the various demands on you which can make the task seem overwhelming. Sometimes you may be asked to make an ethical decision which is a 'choice conflict': you might feel you have to decide where to direct your energies when you are under pressure; you might have to forsake quality for quantity; it might fall to you to sack someone or make them redundant. Often when under unpleasant pressure like this you can resort to a coping mechanism known as 'distancing'. But however much you may try to numb yourself by concentrating on tasks to be done, feelings of distress cannot be dissolved so neatly; if they are not dispersed the anger may turn inward against yourself or outward to unsuspecting, undeserving others.

I found this particularly applicable where Suzy and the Trust were concerned. I had to try to be objective about mistakes she might have made which could have contributed to her disappearance if I was to understand the reality of the problem it indicated within the workplace. However, it was also essential for me to face the personal situation if I was to retain my sanity and cope with the very real grief.

Night work

Apart from the fact that the night is not conducive to work and the daytime often carries with it family and personal responsibilities which interfere with our wish to go to sleep, we do in fact put ourselves 'out of rhythm' when we ask our bodies to work all night.

Internally the body possesses a 'clock' which regulates much of our body's physiology on 24-hour rhythms. Normally these rhythms put us in the waking mode (an increase in body temperature, alertness and mental agility) during the daytime and in the sleep mode (a decrease in body temperature and an increase in fatigue) during the night. Therefore, in a conventional lifestyle there is a matching of rhythmicities between the internal clock and the external environment. This is lost when night work is undertaken.

The following points are worth considering:

- The symptoms indicating difficulty with night work include persistent fatigue, frequent headaches, irritability and gastro-intestinal disorders. If these symptoms are marked and persistent, discuss the matter with a doctor. Note that illnesses unconnected with night work could show similar symptoms.

- The problems, especially in sleeping, are likely to increase with age.

- A good way to adjust to night work is to structure your routine as much as possible. This enables you to achieve objectives rather than feeling tired and sorry for yourself.

    In practice, such structuring can include the following:
    (1) Have regular sleep in surroundings as quiet as possible; if you are woken before the correct time, turn over and try to get back to

sleep. Avoid getting cross. Most of us feel tired about 2 pm so that is a good time to try getting to sleep.

(2) Have regular meals: a large hot meal will structure your work period. Try not to nibble throughout the night.

(3) Structure your leisure time, even though its timing is unusual. Dealing with your husband or boyfriend, children and pets clearly helps here (providing it does not intrude upon sleep); walks or shopping appointments can often be arranged to give a regular structure to your free time.

- Finally, if night work turns out not to be for you, take consolation from the fact that unpleasant symptoms (especially sleep difficulties) seem to stop developing (and generally to recede) when night work is ended.

Change

There are hardly any work areas which do not provide the opportunity for a consistent development and growth in knowledge and practical experience. If you do not feel competent or trained enough to cope with your job, it can result in anxiety and consequently can become a source of stress. Feelings of insecurity can be the result of a change to any new working location, even if only in the same building. They can also occur if you are returning to work after a break.

Try to remember that it is a sign of maturity to be able to admit to yourself and others that there is more to learn, and that self-evaluation and if necessary retraining is an important part of self-development as well as of job satisfaction. Feeling you know all there is to know about a job can actually be an unconscious display of stress showing that you are unsure of how you would cope with change.

Level of responsibility

There has been a great deal of research on the dual problems faced by women in employment. Marilyn Davidson and Cary Cooper's research, *Stress and the Woman Manager* (1983), focused on women in managerial positions. Many of their findings stem from perceptions of the incompatibility of being both female and a leader. They isolated a number of factors which women in managerial positions find particularly stressful:

- They receive far less training in leadership or managerial principles than men; Davidson and Cooper found that women tend to be labelled 'bossy' whereas men are labelled 'leaders'.
- They feel undervalued at the lower end of the managerial hierarchy in comparison with their male colleagues.
- There is not sufficient promotion.
- Top positions in management are mainly occupied by men.
- They find difficulty in being assertive and having confidence in their skills.
- They are more susceptible to role stress because of the multiple demands inherent in running a career and a home/family at the same time.

As Davidson and Cooper say:

'Although this study aims to investigate and isolate the causes and effects of stress in a specific occupational group, that is, women managers, it is important to be conscious of the many extra-organizational sources of stress which can affect the mental and physical health of an individual at work. When investigating the disruption of home and social life as a direct outcome of occupational stress, one has to be aware that there is a feedback loop with stresses at work affecting home and social life, and vice versa.'

They point out too that the socialization of women has contributed to the many problems they have in adjusting to a managerial role:

'Constant emphasis on dependency, nurturance, sacrifice and caring contributes to feelings of ambivalence about self-worth. This lack of self-confidence and esteem can lead to indecisiveness and low risk-taking, which in the long term can result in low achievement motivation. This process can then become a negative circular process, with women . . . not being able to cope with the attitudes and behaviours which are an integral part of the managerial process.'

Home/work conflict

There are sometimes no clear boundaries between work and home. Upset in one area can cause upset in another, and this may be particularly true where the workforce is predominantly female. You may well be a manager at home as well as a manager at work, having almost two full-time jobs. This will be particularly difficult if you are the main carer for children or have elderly dependants at home. Some people have difficulty in switching off from work; others feel that their domestic commitments inhibit their career prospects. This can all become even more difficult if you work at or from home. If this is your problem you must ensure that your physical strength is such that you have the extra energy to cope with the emotional load.

INTERPERSONAL RELATIONSHIPS

Many women feel that they have considerable difficulty in their relations with seniors at work. They describe feelings of distance and isolation from those immediately above them, and problems with the social and emotional support expected from senior staff. They feel a lack of involvement in decision-making and the absence of positive feedback from managers. They try to avoid conflict with senior staff but have an overall feeling that 'management misunderstands my real needs'. Managing demanding clients, members of the public or difficult subordinates can be very stressful. Relationships with colleagues, too, are a potential source of stress.

Stress and resulting tension within an office can arise from:

- *Lack of team cohesion:* Little coordination, teamwork or co-operation between colleagues can lead to reduced effectiveness and diminished job satisfaction.

   Maybe you need to consider how you and your peers treat each other, treat learners, treat helpers. Ask yourself if there is an obvious pecking order. Do you think some people always get a good deal while others don't? Are team members asked for their opinions at relevant times? Do you feel you are treated well by your seniors? Would you feel differently if you were made to feel involved in decision-making rather than being automatically left out?

- *Feelings of isolation:* If everybody works hard but without support from each other, a sense of isolation may result. If you are a junior, you may feel that you are 'just a pair of hands'. If you are in charge, you may feel caught between the more junior staff with less experience and senior managers who seem out of reach. This can increase your feelings of isolation. Everyone else has their own stresses and strains to cope with as well. Sometimes we seem to be running along parallel lines, with little communication between them.

- *Poor communication:* The main problems in interpersonal relationships arise from poor communication. This may be the result of many things, such as lack of clarity, lack of precision, unstructured content or bad timing. It could be just your ineffective listening, or perhaps the use of technical terms, jargon or abbreviations. All these can cause misunderstandings, confusion and mistakes. In the end, your colleagues may not understand what is being demanded of them.

  Another problem in communication involves the tone of what we say. For instance, aggressively spitting out orders heightens tension, whereas overdone charm and manipulation may make people feel irritable and suspicious.

- *Poor feedback:* 'Putting on a brave face' and the 'stiff upper lip' are part of British culture. We often just try to cope. This makes it difficult to ask for and receive help. It may also affect our ability to give help to others.

THE ORGANIZATIONAL CONTEXT

Your role at work and the extent of your responsibility depends on your position within the organization. No one, even a self-employed person, is truly independent. We are all affected by pressures from more powerful influences, the constraints of contractual obligations or the redistribution of resources beyond our control.

We will discuss the part that the organization or employer can play in reducing aggression in the workplace in the final chapter. There are a number of organizational contexts which can contribute to stress and tension in the workforce, for instance:

- *Career:* Many women are worried by having what they consider to be low professional status. Some are frustrated by their limited promotion prospects. Many more suffer stress because of a lack of job satisfaction.

- *Organizational change:* Often a period of change within an organization carries with it alterations in management structure, the types and names of departments and sections, and even sometimes the existing terminology. Change can pose a threat and add to the stress. New people in authority with different roles and new ideas are often felt not to be in tune with those who already see themselves as 'in the know'. Sensitive management of any change process can ease conflict. If you have ever felt personally threatened by changes at work, remember that any changes that *you* wish to implement can be stressful to other colleagues.

- *Managerial problems:* Change can also cause feelings of rift and distance between staff, managers and administration. These feelings may be compounded by the belief that you cannot do anything about the situation, and that decisions have been imposed on you. This can increase your feeling of isolation and a 'them and us' attitude may develop quite unnecessarily. It may well be that in fact these problems have arisen from managers' own responses to the stress in their jobs.

    As employees we can be very reluctant to admit our vulnerability or even to discuss it at work, for fear of the consequences we might have to face. Organizations need to create an atmosphere and structure in which all employees can feel free to express their inability to cope, to discuss their fears and concerns, and to ask for help.

    It is very important for us as employees to be more aware of the characteristics of our work situation which may be responsible for dissatisfaction and/or stress at work . . . Before we can begin to deal with work-related sources of stress, we need to be able to identify them. (Peter Hingley *et al*, research findings on stress in nursing (1986).)

5 Improving your stress management

I hope that by now you are convinced of the link between tension resulting from stress and the likelihood of raised aggression. This is an area in which I know you can do much to help yourself.

COPING MECHANISMS FOR YOU TO DRAW ON

Most of us have immense personal resources for coping with stress. You will probably have developed your own individual set of coping strategies. However, over a period of time, well-established coping mechanisms can become less effective, and over-reliance on or over-use of some methods of coping can in turn cause further problems. The use of drugs for instance: hypnotics to help you sleep, or alcohol to help you relax, can be valuable occasionally but used regularly can lead to addiction. Physical exercise can also be overdone: too much vigorous exercise can cause damage to the heart or joints. You need to have a large choice of coping mechanisms to draw on in order to be able to cope appropriately with each stressful situation.

It is important to try to achieve a balance between the various types of coping methods. Think of the ways in which you deal with stress at the moment, including the many ordinary, everyday ways. Decide which ones you would consider negative, such as getting drunk or kicking the cat. Look at the examples which Meg Bond gave me and see which apply to you or whether you have any to add. These are positive methods of dealing with stress. They come under four headings: active mental or physical distraction, self-nurturance, emotional expression and confronting the problem.

Active mental or physical distraction
- *Hobbies:* gardening, sewing, woodwork, reading, listening to music, crosswords, house plants, chess, cooking, writing letters, do-it-yourself house renovation, upholstery, watching TV, listening to radio, going to the cinema or the theatre.
- *Physical exercise:* walking, jogging, squash, tennis, cycling, digging, golf, swimming, hatha yoga.
- *Chores:* housework, laundry, ironing, mending, washing and polishing the car, chopping wood, shopping.
- *People:* ordinary chitchat with friends, thinking about or helping someone worse off than yourself.

Self-nurturance
- *Rest:* taking proper breaks, ensuring enough sleep, taking cat-naps, relaxation exercises, breathing exercises, meditation, yoga, just putting your feet up, doing nothing, long hot bath or shower, sauna, steam bath, jacuzzi, sunbathing, massage (giving one or having one), getting away from the stressful situation, having a proper holiday.

- *Diet:* having a proper breakfast and lunch, more wholefoods, fewer refined foods, not a lot of any one kind of food (e.g. meat, wheat, coffee, dairy produce), finding out if you have any allergies.

- *Treats:* buying something special, new clothes or hairdo, making a special meal, sex, having a drink, having a cuddle, stroking the dog or cat.

Emotional expression
- *Talking and writing about the stress:* unburdening to a friend/ colleague/pet, having a moan session, telephoning someone, writing down your feelings (e.g. in a letter to a friend), scribbling down feelings in a gush and then tearing it up, joining or starting a support group (e.g. co-counselling).

- *Catharsis:* having a good cry, bashing, knocking or throwing cushions, punching a punchbag, shaking, yelling at the dog or cat, stamping your feet, screaming or shouting into a pillow, swearing loudly, smashing or ripping up something not valuable (e.g. cardboard box, cracked crockery, old clothes).

- *Creative emotional expression:* poetry, painting and drawing, writing short stories, sculpture, singing, making music, amateur dramatics, dancing.

Confronting the problem
- *Thinking:* working it through step by step, pinpointing and analysing the problem, clarifying the causes of the stress, brain-storming solutions, deciding what you really want or need, deciding priorities, making a plan, getting the information you need for dealing with it.

- *Other people:* asking for help or advice, asserting your wants and needs, challenging someone if they are causing the stress.

- *The organization or system:* telling people in power (e.g. managers, MP) your opinions, giving them any information they need to help make a case for change, starting or joining a joint action group, joining a pressure group (e.g. peace group, union).

Underline the methods on these lists which you use. Consider which categories are stronger and which are weaker, those you use often and those you seldom use. See which methods of dealing with stress you would most like to develop or use more often in order to achieve a more balanced repertoire of coping mechanisms.

If one or more of the categories is less well represented or less often used than the others, there may be an imbalance in your coping mechanisms which could lead to further stress. For instance, if you pay little attention to self-nurturance or distraction, you may exhaust yourself. If emotional expression is lacking, you could have problems arising from emotional repression. If you seldom confront problems, then avoidance can lead to an escalation of pressure. And so on.

Understanding emotions

Emotions seem to be unwelcome in the workplace. We tend to consider emotional maturity as the absence of our emotions rather than our skill in being aware of them and expressing them appropriately. We applaud the control of emotions rather than encouraging them. We see 'getting emotional' as a failure, while perhaps being 'rational' is over-valued. Emotions are subjective and we may write them off as worthless, whereas we see reason as objective and therefore 'right'. We need to think of emotions as socially acceptable. At the moment certain emotions are listed as signs and symptoms of mental illness, but seldom is an emotion acknowledged to be a sign of mental health.

It is hardly a wonder that we learn to keep our emotions to ourselves. We ignore them and hope they will go away!

At work we strive to hide our emotions, and this puts a severe strain on us. It is a negative way of dealing not only with our emotions, but also with other people. Emotions are a great resource which can help us to cope with our own stress and other people's as well. We should regard them as resources which, with understanding and skill, we can use to our advantage.

Defences can lead us to bottle up our feelings, so that we gradually build up a backlog of repressed emotions. Triggers in our everyday life can stir up these unexpressed feelings, and bring responses which are over-reactions or under-reactions to the real situation. This is unhelpful for our health and relationships, and it will cause further stress.

- *Physical reactions* The anger hormone noradrenalin prepares the body for the fight response which when not expressed results in physical tension. This is particularly noticeable in the shoulders, arms and jaw (we even talk of irritating people being 'a pain in the neck'). The fear hormone adrenalin leaves residual tension in the legs and chest, and unexpressed grief leaves tension in the chest and abdomen. Many illnesses are now being associated with repressed emotions. Repressed anger, for instance, is considered a significant factor in the development of cancer in women.

- *Mental reactions* These can include mental blocks (Suzy did this with exams); impaired concentration, decision-making and logical thinking; forgetfulness.

- *Effects on behaviour* Under stress you may fall back on rigid, distorted patterns of behaviour which might be your habitual way of attempting to cope but which are inappropriate to the situation, or perhaps ineffective and out of date. You might, for example, placate or avoid any hint of conflict, or set yourself up to fail (for instance by setting yourself an impossible target) or to be put down or perhaps taken advantage of; unconsciously you might choose the wrong type of person as a friend or partner, or not allow someone who is suffering to express their feelings.

- *Emotional effects* Our defence mechanisms not only bottle up our uncomfortable emotions, they smother positive feelings too. If we allow ourselves to become so adept at holding back our negative feelings all the time we are likely to become numb in situations where positive emotions would naturally come through. We will lose our ability to show love, care, delight, pleasure and so on. This numbness will tend to alternate with emotional outbursts. The 'last straw' syndrome will develop, where we hit out verbally or physically at ourselves or other innocent people, over-reacting to real or imagined misdeeds. It is as if the pressure builds up so much in the emotional bottle that the cork flies and too much comes rushing out at once. We then become the aggressors.

- *Stress and self-awareness* It is because of this misuse that emotions have got a bad name, a sort of 'all-or-nothing' expectation. We need to accept and understand emotions, building into our culture more opportunities for developing them and for using our emotional skills.

SKILLS WHICH CAN HELP

Skills have to be learned, practised and practised again so that eventually you will put them into use automatically.

- *Calming yourself down:* Breathing properly can be an excellent aid whenever you feel anxious or tense. It is vital to concentrate on breathing *out* – you will then expel all the air and create a vacuum which will refill as a reflex action. If you concentrate on breathing *in* your tension is likely to increase and the muscles of your chest contract, making breathing more difficult and leading you, under extreme pressure, to hyperventilate.

Let your breath go without breathing in first
Take a deep slow breath and hold it briefly
Breathe out slowly, like a deep sigh
Drop your shoulders
Unclench your hands
Drop your jaw – and purse your lips slightly
Count to ten slowly
When you speak make sure you speak slowly and in a low tone

This will calm your listener down as well as yourself. I found this invaluable for media work.

LOOKING AFTER YOUR PHYSICAL CONDITION

Diet and exercise

Understanding the physiology of stress enables you to see that you can alleviate the long-term health problems it causes by improving your diet and increasing exercise. Chronic stress results in the prolonged release of nutrients, glucose and fatty acids which are not normally used up by the sublimated stress response, bringing undesirable side-effects. The unused fat, for instance, can be laid down in the arterial walls. This can be partially counteracted by sensible nutrient intake and increased exercise. Exercise in particular uses up this source of energy released into the bloodstream.

Hormone levels

Changes in hormone levels can increase feelings of stress, particularly premenstrually or during the menopause. They can also reduce your ability to cope with stressful situations. These effects can be countered in such a way as to help not only you but everyone around you, as those who have been on the receiving end of your irritation and outbursts will be quick to agree. It makes sense to consult your doctor rather than suffering nobly. I am sure that the fact that my hormones seem to have settled down after the menopause has been an enormously helpful bonus over the months of added trauma and pressure.

Sleeping well

Soon after my daughter Suzy disappeared I consulted a psychiatrist friend, who is a renowned worldwide authority on anxiety. 'How shall I survive?' I asked him. 'Well, one of the most vital elements is sleep,' he said. 'Work yourself so hard that you fall asleep out of sheer exhaustion.' I followed his advice to the letter and it worked. Sleep is essential to your well-being. Without it you become tense and nervous; when you are anxious and stressed you may suffer from insomnia. It can become a vicious circle. Sleep not only refreshes the body; it also, through dreams, restores the mind and discharges tension. We used to wake up with tears streaming down our faces – it was very therapeutic.

The body works on a 24-hour cycle (everyone has their own inner clock known as a circadian rhythm) – a cycle in which a 90- to 120-minute period of sleep – or wakefulness – alternates with a five- to ten-minute dream period. This goes on unceasingly twenty-four hours a day, and it is reflected in a similar rise and fall of the body's temperature. The highest points are when you feel most alive and alert, the lowest are when you are daydreaming. It is much easier to get to sleep during one of the low points in temperature; it is worth trying to keep track of these and, if possible, to adjust your sleep pattern accordingly.

When you fall asleep the eyelids close and the pupils become small. Breathing is diminished, blood pressure falls, the heart slows down, the temperature drops and the digestive juices and saliva decrease. There are several stages from drowsiness to oblivious sleep, when all the muscles are relaxed and it is difficult to be woken. A normal person automatically changes position from twenty to sixty times a night. The brain still receives every sound and touch but though it responds it does not express the messages in conscious actions (except in sleepwalking).

There are two kinds of sleep – slow-wave sleep (which is dreamless and usually starts the sleeping sequence) and dreaming sleep, known as REM (rapid eye movement). The two types alternate throughout the night. You will suffer little if you are deprived of slow-wave sleep, but without REM you are likely to suffer increased tension and nervous reaction. REM sleep is the deepest and most refreshing; it is good for your mental health as it restores the central nervous system (though how this is achieved is not yet clear). Alcohol, barbiturates or tranquillizers all decrease the amount of REM sleep, and after taking them you may wake up feeling depressed and tired.

We all have times when our minds seem to be racing or very tense. I am lucky to have advice from Joe Macdonald Wallace on this and to have practised his sleep exercises for many years.

If you are longing for a good night's sleep but find yourself tossing and turning, wide-awake yet tired, what steps can you take to help yourself clear your racing mind? You might be busy reliving the minutiae of the day past, apprehensively surveying the day to come, or perhaps just worrying over details of almost no significance at all. First of all, you must understand that your mental activity may well have triggered off a 'red-alert' response. In that case it will be beneficial to get up and move around – to the bathroom or the kitchen – and then when you have cooled off and calmed down go back to bed and make yourself comfortable. Then quite deliberately:

- visualize a room or a place where you feel safe and at home.
- look around slowly and see its objects and features (or people if you have placed them there).
- look around again faster this time.
- repeat for a third time.
- choose one point (an object, person or point) and, keeping your eyes fixed, try to think your way around.
- do not let your eyes move (go back to the beginning if they do) and repeat the thinking around.
- you will fall asleep (if you do not cheat)!

The thinking process is to a great extent a muscular process, involving visualization of images, and verbalization, or self-speech. We all use both, but people tend to one extreme or the other. You will recognize the 'visualizers' as they speak or listen to you, their eyes rolling rapidly in the sockets, trying to pluck images out of the air. Most visualizers cease to think when their eyes become fixed. An easy illustration is to think of the number of people who fall fast asleep in front of television, especially when the eyeline is static, and even more so when the viewer is concentrating hard and really wants to hear and know what is being said! A lecturer can have the same effect.

The 'verbalizers' talk to themselves overtly to solve their problems, and are usually unaware that they are doing it.

People who cannot sleep at night because 'their minds won't relax' are often, in fact, keeping themselves awake by the muscular activity of visualization and verbalization feeding back into the brain, maintaining a measurable amount of heightened arousal of the central nervous system which in the end influences other systems and organs. This makes it impossible to arrive at the reduction of electrocortical activity that is essential for sleep.

1 *Relaxing the muscles of visualization*
As this has to be practised with eyes closed, read the instructions first, then close your eyes and try it out.

With the eyelids lightly closed, move your eyes (but not your head) left and right, up and down, until you are clearly conscious of the eyes moving, and perhaps even conscious of the tensions in the ocular muscles. Now let the eye muscles relax so that the eyeballs are flopped down in the sockets, with no movement at all. This is difficult, for you may have to overcome many years of defensive habit, but with practice it can be done. When the eye muscles are completely relaxed you cannot visualize, so one aspect of the restless mind is blocked.

2 *Relaxing the muscles of verbalization*
Speech may involve some thirty-five different muscles. When you shout, they are strongly contracted; when you whisper, their tension is diminished; when you speak inwardly without any sound at all, there is still tension in many muscles leading to brain arousal and involvement of the autonomic nervous system as in visualization. The autonomic nervous system controls the automatic body actions which are directed by the unconscious; for instance, you do not tell your heart to beat nor your finger to scratch your nose if you feel an itch.

Read the instructions first, then practise with your eyes closed so that you can pay attention to what is happening in the muscles.

First, recite aloud any nursery rhyme or poem that you know. Note how the muscles of the jaw, the lips, the tongue, under the chin and in the throat are all involved. Now recite again, speaking inwardly only to yourself, and again note how these muscles contract – only minutely, but they are still feeding back impulses to the brain. Now try to relax these muscles of speech – in the jaws, the lips, the tongue and the throat – as completely as possible. When you can do this, self-speech as an aspect of mental activity is impossible. So with the eye muscles completely relaxed, and the muscles of speech completely relaxed, your mind can no longer be restless.

Alternatives to this method include two tranquillizing pills or two double scotches, but these are much more costly, both in money and health.

Learning to meditate

Meg Bond uses Whitehill's (1980) definition of meditation as 'a process of contemplation directing the attention of the conscious mind toward an inner experience or outwards to something which is perceived outside the self'. This sounds esoteric, but there is no doubt in my mind that meditation can aid stress reduction by helping to produce a state of relaxed awareness. It can also lower the blood pressure dramatically. It does need to be taught and mastered. Many Local Education Authorities run classes.

There is another form of meditation which can be mastered on your own and which can give you a positive result. You need to be quiet and peaceful, and to be able to lie down in comfort and safety. Close your eyes and gently place your palms on your stomach (below the waist), breathe in until you feel your hands rise and continue until you can take in no more air, hold the position and then allow the air to come rushing out, hold for a moment and then repeat. When you feel really relaxed, your mind will find itself free and maybe even a trifle bored! Now rehearse in your mind a skill you want to practise; go through the imagined movements carefully one by one until completed. You may be surprised at the effect this has on your performance. American tennis players use this method to great advantage.

Communication skills

In the next chapters I will give you two ways in which you can improve on your communication skills. This can have a dual effect on stress reduction. It enables your opinion, message or instruction to be transmitted with clarity, direction and in a more structured way, so you are more likely to be successful. It can also help the receivers, enabling them to improve their understanding; they will know where they are going and what is being demanded of them; their anxiety about the unknown will be reduced. It can also help you to say no to an unreasonable demand. This will not only lead you towards a realistic expectation of your own role and that of others; it will also improve your self-image and confidence.

A few more ideas

Animals can help: dogs are companions, and stroking a cat's fur can bring down blood pressure. Our two dogs and Burmese and half-Abyssinian cats are an immense source of comfort and help. Gardening can be most satisfying – fulfilling our natural urge to till, grow and look after. Sex too can play its part. As a doctor in Hong Kong told the colony's Financial Women's Association, 'Sex is a good antidote to stress and tension.' But, he added, 'The only problem is its inaccessibility in certain situations such as a traffic jam!' The Tension Control Technique might prove more useful.

TENSION CONTROL TECHNIQUE

Memorizing a 'technique' sounds difficult but in fact as you gradually become familiar with the moves and routine of TCT (Tension Control Technique) the body will begin to respond automatically and eventually you will find yourself putting the technique into operation when needed, without conscious thought. However, this eventual result does not just happen. It takes some concentration, time and thought to master the skill. For a skill it is: relaxation is not for most of us a natural habit, so it has to be learned. But it is worth the effort. To make it easy we will take it step by step:

- The first week you should concentrate on reading and 'doing' the technique.
- You should then progress to thinking and recognizing tension and release.
- By then you should be able to remember and feel the tension release.
- Next you should practise continually, and consciously apply the tension release during 'stress moments'.
- TCT should become almost automatic.
- You can then also try the sleep exercises, deep meditation/ relaxation, and massage as well.

The Tension Control Technique we use in Slimnastics works on the premise that only a fully contracted muscle will fully relax when it is released; and that as tight muscles signal to the brain that there is an 'alert' to be responded to, relaxed muscles have the opposite effect. It is a simple straightforward idea; the beauty of it is that it works! To release any tension you have in your body, work steadily from the top to the toes, clenching the groups of muscles tightly, holding them and then releasing completely. Give yourself time to really feel the tension and then savour the relaxation with each move.

Before you start you will need to make sure you are in a position to be able to relax without any effort. You should be able to breathe easily (no constricting clothes or slumped position) and have time for uninterrupted concentration. Allow yourself at least ten minutes, if possible completely alone.

Prop the book open on a table at a distance you can comfortably read. Find a chair with an upright back in which you can sit easily, facing the book; your back and shoulders should be supported, your knees slightly apart, slightly rolled outwards, and your feet flat on the ground. If you have short legs put your feet on a stool or otherwise raise them so that you can completely release the tension in your legs. Let your arms hang loosely with your hands on your lap. Now read through and follow the instructions slowly. Remember to keep breathing easily and regularly throughout.

- *Start at the forehead* Wrinkle up the skin and frown between the eyebrows . . . hold it . . . let go and release. Frown more deeply causing deep wrinkles . . . hold it . . . let go and release. Now frown hard, involve the whole scalp, feel the tightness . . . hold hard . . . release completely, feel the tension in the scalp relax.

- *Now for the eyes* Screw them up just slightly, feel the wrinkles at the sides . . . hold it . . . let go and release. Screw them up more tightly until there is only a pinprick of light . . . hold . . . and release. Screw them up tightly until the nose and forehead are involved . . . hold hard . . . let go completely.

- *On to the mouth* Pull sideways slightly . . . feel the tension . . . release. Pull the mouth into a smile . . . hold it . . . let go and release completely. Draw the mouth into a grimace . . . hold it hard . . . let go and relax.

- *Now the jaw* Clench the teeth together . . . now release. Clench the teeth and the jaw very tightly . . . feel the tension . . . release completely so that the jaw drops, the mouth opens and the tongue falls back.

- *Next the shoulders* Lift slightly, hold . . . now drop. Raise the shoulders higher . . . hold them . . . release and let them fall back. Lift the shoulders to the ears . . . hold hard, let them go and feel the tension release.

- *On to the hands* Clench the hands into a fist and feel your fingernails in the palm . . . hold . . . and release. Clench the hands hard until the knuckles show white and you feel the tension in the shoulders . . . hold hard . . . let go and feel the tension release.

- *Now your trunk* Push the small of your back into the chair and feel the abdomen tighten and your pelvis move . . . hold . . . and release. Repeat, making the movement stronger . . . hold longer . . . let go completely and feel yourself sink into the chair.

- *Down to your feet* Push your heels into the ground, feel the tension in the calves and thighs . . . hold . . . let go. Press down hard . . . hold tight . . . release completely.

- *Continue to sit* for a moment concentrating on breathing in and expanding, holding the breath briefly and then expelling as a release.

When you have mastered the commands and responses, it might help to lie down in warmth and comfort (a pillow under your neck and knees if you wish) and at the start:

- lift your head and look at your toes . . . feel the tension and release . . . repeat.
- start at the toes and tighten your calves, buttocks, hands, shoulders, face, hold and release . . . repeat.
- now close your eyes and think of nothing but yourself while you go through the routine slowly and steadily.

As you become more practised you will begin to be aware whenever your muscles are under tension, and you will naturally tense and release them. There will be times when you need to take the actions deliberately, and that is when you will be really amazed at the results – such as a clear mind, quicker thought and the ability to master tricky situations without producing aggression on either side.

CHAPTER 2

Attitudes

Consultants:

STEVIE HOLLAND
Polytechnic of the South Bank

MARCIA REYNOLDS
Management consultant

All passages indicated by marginal arrows are directly derived from Jean Orr, 'Managing Aggression', Workbook and Reader for the Distance Learning Centre, Polytechnic of the South Bank, London, 1987, except where otherwise indicated.

I saw in a magazine a very odd definition of the word 'attitude', referring to the black urban American meaning – touch, savvy, hip. This threw me into confusion until I found that the *Oxford Dictionary* described 'attitude' as 'posture, pose, disposition, behaviour'. This is what I am going to discuss in this chapter. I want us to consider how other people come over to us, the signals and messages they present and how we react; as well as the unconscious reflections of their attitudes that we can pass back.

I have been helped a great deal by Stevie Holland and Jean Orr, by Lynne Howells and by Desmond Morris's field guide to human behaviour, *Manwatching*, which is a most useful and readable book. Marcia Reynolds was my teacher in the section on role-playing.

When we say that we understood or felt the 'vibes' from someone, we are not talking about extrasensory perception. Just like animals, we communicate with each other all the time. Understanding body language is extremely useful in the quest to manage aggression. Many unwritten and unconsciously accepted 'rules' can lead to tension and consequent feelings of anger if they are transgressed. Some attitudes are threatening; some will defuse aggression.

The last chapter was about aggression in yourself and others and the resulting stress and tension. I hope you now understand the necessity of relaxation to combat this aggression effectively and that you are taking every opportunity to practise the Tension Control Technique. Use it frequently throughout the day and it will gradually, except in times of real trauma, become instinctive and automatic. Being calm will also help you to have a clear mind to consider our next topic – social attitudes and their effect on aggression.

This part of the book is about being aware of your own attitudes, comparing them with those you meet. It is about discovering how you feel when faced with certain attitudes. Decide whether you should modify or alter your own non-verbal communication. Look in the mirror and see how you come over.

1 Non-verbal communication

Non-verbal communication means all forms of human communication not controlled by speech. It also includes non-verbal aspects of speech, known as paralanguage, such as meanings communicated by the tone of your voice, the speed and pitch. For instance, if you say 'That talk was most interesting' in a flat, clipped voice, it will convey a different meaning than if you had said it with emphasis and variety in the tone. 'Paralanguage' also refers to the sounds we make which have meaning but are not words. For example we say 'mm-hmm', 'aha', 'uh-huh', in order to show that we are listening, though we may not speak.

We send out and receive information about the people we meet by a whole range of non-verbal communication. First, we get an impression from their general appearance. Unconsciously we may weigh up a number of options. Are they tidy or ill-kempt; are they formally or casually dressed; are they wearing badges that say something about their political beliefs; do they look well cared for? We often draw generalized conclusions based on appearance, but we need to be wary: while appearance will tell us something about a person, we must remember the danger of labelling or stereotyping someone unfairly.

Secondly, we receive an impression of a person's mood from the way they hold their body. People who are anxious may clench their hands, pull at their clothing, adjust their hair; they may have difficulty sitting still, may frown and bite their lips or perform other nervous movements such as fiddling with a pen or watch. Someone who is depressed may sit slumped in a chair, looking downcast and refusing to respond to conversation.

We receive a wide range of non-verbal information, probably more than we realize. We also tell others about ourselves, probably more than we wish to admit. We need to be sensitive to these aspects of communication and recognize that even before we speak we have probably conveyed messages that will have a fundamental impact on the other person.

Non-verbal communication can contradict your spoken word. You may be saying 'No' and nodding your head to indicate 'Yes', or saying 'I want to do this' but shaking your head to say 'No'. You might be saying 'I feel fine' when your whole body shows that you are tense and anxious. You may show discrepancies between your eyes and mouth, so that when you smile your eyes stay dull. When these contradictory messages appear the non-verbal message is said to be telling the truth.

TYPES OF NON-VERBAL COMMUNICATION

Body contact

It is through body contact that we express a large range of meaning from the close proximity of lovers to the fleeting contact of shaking hands with a stranger. We have unspoken, unwritten rules about body contact which vary between cultures. For example, the French often kiss each other. Turkish men not only kiss each other but walk with their arms round each other, which in Britain would not be appropriate behaviour. Touch has an important communicating role, showing encouragement, concern and emotional support. It can be used to help people who are in distress, anxious or are having difficulty articulating their feelings.

Sometimes people in caring professions can keep too great a distance between themselves and their clients, afraid that they will be seen as 'unprofessional'. When clients are very distressed it is often difficult to know what to say, but it may be enough to touch them and convey a message of concern through our body language. In situations like this it is useful just to make physical contact with the individual by, for example, touching her arm, taking her hand, or putting an arm around her shoulder.

However, you should always be aware that some people may be distressed by touch. They may feel sexually threatened or they may have unpleasant memories of being touched. A woman who has been sexually assaulted or harassed may be distressed by body contact, especially if it comes from a man. Sometimes it may be necessary to ask if it is all right to touch. You are more likely to respond in an appropriate manner if you take your cue from non-verbal language.

Orientation

The distance between you and another person is very important, and the position you adopt will affect the relationship. Sitting side by side is seen as cooperative, whereas sitting opposite implies competitiveness and can be seen as authoritarian. Business people often talk of eyeball-to-eyeball confrontation! For conversation or consultation it is best to sit at a 90-degree angle, preferably with no desks or barriers in between. It is also counterproductive to be at a different height, as to be higher is seen as 'superior' and does not set the scene for good communication. It will help if you sit at the same level or even a little lower so that the other person feels superior or at least equal.

Personal space

It can feel aggressive, even offensive, if someone comes too close to you (this of course does not apply to your loved ones or those you know very well). You can probably think of people who seem to crowd you.

As you feel them getting too close you may move back, then they follow until you are backed up against the wall! Why do you feel like this?

Imagine you have an area around you shaped like an egg with the pointed end in front. When someone gets too close they are entering this private space. Anyone invading this mobile personal territory is threatening its occupier and will create immediate tension.

If we have to get too close, as we do for instance on the tube, we tend not to face other people, turning sideways and avoiding eye contact. If accidental eye contact occurs, we probably quickly turn away. If someone stares, we begin to feel threatened.

If you were on an empty train or bus, it would feel very odd if someone were to sit beside you when plenty of other seats were available. In that sort of situation we often extend our private space, using something like a bag or a briefcase as a barrier between ourselves and the other person.

Personal territory refers to the wider areas in which we seek to establish a sense of security and belonging. All of us establish personal territory. It might be at home, where we may have a certain area which is seen as ours, or at work where we arrange our office in a way which makes us feel secure. Some people defend their territory by keeping a desk between themselves and others – a teacher may feel most comfortable distanced behind a table or rostrum. At a party we may use a glass as a barrier between ourselves and others who crowd us. In defending personal territory barriers are often set up which hinder effective communication and interaction. For example, a teacher might achieve more participation with students in a circle without desks.

When visiting people at home it is important to be aware of this personal territory. It can be threatening when someone in authority makes a visit, particularly if the visitor appears to be judgmental, officious and does not respect the client's privacy by acting at all times as a guest in his home. It is vital to remember that, for instance, a female social worker going into a client's home may be petrified by his anger, but she still has the power to take away his kids. Both will be under threat, so the right personal distance is essential.

Proximity means how close people are to each other. We all respond to an invisible line between ourselves and others. If you are too far back the other person can feel inaccessible and you will not be effectual. Too close, and the other person may become uncomfortable and try to move away. People can have differing optimum distances and what feels too close for one person may be fine for someone else. When standing we can interact at a closer distance than when we are sitting.

A sitting distance of five to six feet is usual for work situations though eight to ten feet is the norm at home. When standing, the normal space is about three to four feet. Proximity is related to status: often a person of higher status feels free to approach a lower-status person, but not vice versa. Your boss may feel free to stand closer to you, as a worker, than you feel able to stand to your boss.

Facial expression

Facial expressions teach us a lot about each other. We can often understand what someone is feeling or thinking. We use statements such as 'She couldn't face me', 'His face was a picture', 'It was written all over his face'. This shows us how important facial expression is in showing anger, guilt, fear or joy. Our eyes and mouth are probably the most expressive, and indeed may give out contradictory messages. It is quite possible for you to smile with your mouth but not your eyes, or to look interested with your eyes while stifling a yawn. You can demonstrate anxiety, fear or embarrassment in your facial expression although you say you are fine. Your facial expression is probably showing your true feelings. Remember that others may be watching you closely for your reaction to what they say.

Eye contact

Throughout language and literature there are many references to the importance we place on eye contact: 'He couldn't look me in the eye', 'Eyes are the windows of the soul', 'He is shifty-eyed'. The more intimate we are with a person the more eye contact we have. 'They gazed into each other's eyes' is an expression applied to lovers.

Although you are probably unaware of it, there are 'rules' which govern eye contact. The speaker will usually look away from the listener, but will establish direct eye contact from time to time to make sure that she is being heard. Frequently when the speaker is concentrating on what she is saying eye contact can be minimal, but when she is getting ready to finish, more frequent eye contact can be a signal for the listener to respond or to start speaking herself. If the speaker does not establish at least some eye contact she may be distressed and uncomfortable about what she is saying. I was very conscious of this when I was being interviewed after Suzy disappeared. Every time I found my eyes sliding away I realized I was distressed and this avoiding action was helping me to keep my cool.

A listener tends to look at the speaker during the conversation and will look away when bored. It is very difficult to maintain a conversation when a listener does not look attentive. Even the most articulate and talkative people tend to dry up in the absence of any response. This is also true in group situations when one person starts to talk and stops because no one is paying attention. You have probably experienced this at a meeting or dinner party.

When someone is talking we demonstrate clearly that we are listening by using appropriate eye contact. The important word here is 'appropriate'. If, for instance, we maintain continual eye contact it can be interpreted as threatening and may precipitate violence. You have probably heard people in potentially violent situations asking aggressively, 'What are you staring at?'

The status difference also occurs in eye contact. Those who consider themselves superior maintain longer eye contact than those of lower status. This does, however, vary between the sexes. Usually women, especially of Asian cultures, are expected to lower their eyes first.

The appropriate use of eye contact is of vital importance for interaction, but we do occasionally find ourselves in circumstances when eye contact feels uncomfortable. It may sometimes be easier to focus on a point just above the bridge of the nose. This gives the impression of eye contact but may be easier to maintain in difficult situations.

Hand and head movements

When we communicate, body movements play an important part in giving messages. Fidgeting hands and clenched fists show the mood of the person. Gestures which can denote anxiety include playing with the hair, rubbing the face, fiddling with a pen or watch, or tapping the feet. There is a wide range of gestures with acquired meanings in our society, and the meanings vary in other cultures.

As we pick up messages about other people, so they understand things about us. If, for instance, we strongly disapprove of something said to us we draw back or fold our arms, look aggressive or find an excuse to get up and move away. Look carefully at your own body movements. They may have just become habits. You might want to change behaviour patterns which are distracting or revealing. You can probably recall someone who annoys you with a habit or movement. Sometimes these movements seem to be catching and you find yourself compulsively imitating them.

It can be useful to see yourself on video. Although you might find it painful at least it makes it possible to be honest with yourself about your habits. Alternatively, you could ask a good friend to tell you about your faults (as well as your strengths). I watch myself very carefully every time I appear on television and do my best to 'right the wrongs' – I often forget the next time but it is still very useful.

Social behaviour

From a very early age, perhaps from the moment we are born, we are socialized – that is, we learn behaviour which labels us 'female' and different from the male. We have dolls, they have cars; we learn that it is all right for us to cry but we also, whether we like it or not, learn the role of 'carer': fetching the plaster and cleaning up a wound, cooking the meal, mending the sock, doing the shopping. We know we will bear the children and nurture them while we work. Most of us also learn that we have the privilege of having a door opened for us, of going first into a room, of being helped into a car and many other small politenesses. In the workplace, however, such actions can become very dangerous indeed. Our social behaviour may have no place in our working lives.

As far as we can understand, Suzy followed her normal pattern that working day. She showed a strange man into a house which was empty, had no electricity, no telephone. She unlocked the door and automatically preceded her client. With the door shut behind them she could have been trapped. It may well be that you should rethink your behaviour patterns and be aware of those which could lead you into trouble.

'Good manners' – or social behaviour, call it what you will – can work the other way around as well. A tall, good-looking architect told me a story of how when she was a young girl working in Paris her room was suddenly invaded by what she described as a 'rampant' male. Without thinking she said, 'Well, as you are here you might as well sit down.' He automatically sat, she tipped up the chair, strode over him and out of the door! A similar thing happened when I bumped my car into what I took to be a Telecom van which appeared round the back of our road in rather a hurry. I jumped out and asked for their address as I would have to inform the insurance company. Without thinking, because they wanted to get away, they gave it to me and left. They were, in fact, three burglars who had given their correct address and were caught with all their booty. In both cases, these men were undone by their social behaviour.

2 Role-play

Communication systems abound within the workfield –'Just take a letter, Miss Brown', 'Give us a ring with your answer', 'Fax the information through'. These are endless messages going from one place to another. Computers are informing computers – printers pour out knowledge from other printers, but all to no avail if the human receiving the information does not 'connect' with the one who is communicating.

How many times have we said to ourselves, 'I simply did not understand him', 'Our lines were crossed', 'We are not on the same wavelength', 'It's all jargon to me'. I had never realized before just how apt these descriptions are of occasions when we fail to achieve that two-way connection which is necessary in order to understand and be understood. Nor had I appreciated before just how much this failure can foster, aggravate or provoke aggression between two parties.

We can all probably think of times when we felt that tension rising in ourselves because we could not get our point across, or were being patronized, talked at, or were at cross purposes. However, we could go a long way to reducing aggression in our working lives if we looked at the other side of the coin and considered whether we ourselves are effective communicators or, perhaps, are unwittingly creating problems.

It was a delight when I discovered Transactional Analysis (TA), as in my innocence I had previously put it to one side as being introspective and rather 'over the top'. I had failed to see that it is a straightforward analysis of communication which defines ways in which we can relate constructively to others. It provides an objective view of our attitudes and behaviour and those of our colleagues.

Transactional Analysis was developed by Eric Berne, a Canadian psychiatrist. It is taught by many people using a variety of techniques. I chose Marcia Reynolds, an American living in Great Britain and a leading authority on the subject. She has now become a management consultant and claims that much of her success is due to her knowledge of TA.

There are, of course, many obvious reasons why we fail to communicate effectively with our fellow beings. These range from social class to language, accent or even mannerisms. They can stem from differences in ethnic or cultural background, religious beliefs or values. Some women feel intimidated by men and some men are dismissive of women or occasionally demoralized by them. Mental confusion, illness, tiredness, pain, emotional disease, lack of concentration or a sense of self-worth can all stand in the way of understanding. It takes confidence to realize that other people may experience similar problems.

Apart from problems like these, which can hamper our communication with others, we may also assume roles that can prove unhelpful. We may automatically play a 'part' or allow an aspect of our personality to take over at an inopportune moment. Though they present difficulties in our interactions with others, these behaviours can also help us to analyse the roles that people play. We can then begin to notice when our behaviour is helpful or unhelpful in the work situation. This is the essence of Transactional Analysis.

THE PARENTAL ROLE

The parental role can take two forms, described in TA terms as the Controlling Parent and the Nurturing Parent. When you observe yourself feeling, thinking or acting as you saw your parents or other authority figures act when you were a child, you are behaving like a Parent. You are assuming your Parent Role when you give advice, criticize, discipline, moralize, nurture, protect, make rules and regulations, teach and judge.

- *Controlling Parent*: The typical picture of the Controlling Parent is the moralistic, judgmental, authoritarian figure with a scowling face and set jaw who points his finger and says 'Because I said so', 'You ought . . .'. This is almost a caricature of a boss figure, but it is quite recognizable even in ourselves, particularly when we are playing a part in which we lack complete confidence. On the other hand it can give clear and firm guidance, control and direction when required.

- *Nurturing Parent*: The typical picture of the Nurturing Parent is of a caring, permissive, supportive, understanding person who is warm and sympathetic. This boss would pat us on the back, smile and say 'Well done', 'Don't worry', 'I'll sort it out for you'. This role, adopted by others, helps us to feel comfortable with ourselves and probably to work better; however, the Controlling Parent might have to emerge to take responsibility for a final decision or to make a judgment.

THE ADULT ROLE

When you observe yourself dealing with facts, analysing situations coldly and logically and making decisions based on current reality, you are using your Adult Role. The Adult part of you functions like a computer, processing information and gathering data but without feeling. Your Adult Role is not related in any way to your age. You use it when you store information, plan, check alternatives, reason, recall and evaluate, estimate probabilities and set limits.

When you are assuming your Adult Role you will be open and level, appearing confident and calm. Your behaviour will be thoughtful, alert and straight and you will use words such as 'Correct', 'How?', 'Why and Where?'. It is easy to see that the Adult is a very useful role and a valuable member of a management team. However, when you use this behaviour you disregard the human need for caring and nurturing, and you will not be much fun. The Adult is factually orientated, and you will work at your best in the role when you use your Parent judgments as information, and utilize the intuitive guesses which come from your Child Role.

THE CHILD ROLE

Allowing your Child Role to take over can be useful in a multitude of situations. You can learn to use humour to relax tense situations. You can learn to acknowledge your emotions to yourself and to use them as a barometer to pace your discussion and actions at work. Your Child Role can be most useful in interpersonal relationships and can help you to make your work more productive.

The Child Role contains all the feelings and impulses that are natural in an infant, along with your recordings of your early experiences, reactions to them and the learned view of yourself and others. It is in this role that you invent, create ways to compromise and find alternatives. It is usually aided by Adult facts or Adult reasoning. In this role you will observe yourself expressing anger, fear, rebelliousness, curiosity, trust, love, excitement, self-indulgence, aggression or servility. There are several variations of this Child Role:

- *The Natural Child*: In this role you will show the spontaneous, fun-loving, energetic, genuine and curious side of your nature. You will use words which show high feeling, you will allow yourself to enjoy your senses and be uninhibited. This part of you can also be disruptive and interrupt serious problem-solving. Your Natural Child Role does occasionally need some Parental Control!

  A variant of this Natural Child Role is called the Little Professor because in this role you will be at your most creative and intuitive. This is the role which instinctively paces other people; knows how to reach them on their own wavelength; understands when to joke and when to ask for tasks to be done; knows the needs of others and uses creative ways to ensure work is accomplished well. The Little Professor can also be sly and manipulative. Pulling strings is a favourite method for the Little Professor to get its way!

- *The Adapted Child*: In this role you can be defiant, rebellious and complaining, or passive and delaying. The Adapted Child can show a quivering lip, moist eyes and appear sad, pouting or coy. This is the part of you which has learned the social skills using such phrases as 'Please can I?', 'I wish', 'Sorry'. A variant is the Compliant Child who will always arrive on time and leave on time even if it would prefer to do otherwise. It will comply without thinking or questioning, rather than taking the lead in any situation. The Adapted Child Role has also learned the feeling of embarrassment and will often keep quiet to avoid looking stupid. The Rebellious Child variant can emerge when an individual starts to become self-directed and begins to know what he or she wants to do; or it could stubbornly go against an idea purely as a signal of rebellion rather than judgment. It is the Adapted Child which holds a grudge, whereas the Natural Child does not know how to retain bad feelings.

It is important to realize that our personalities are made up of all these roles. When you act, speak or make gestures that are influenced by your parents' behaviour, you are taking on the role of the Parent. The Child in you influences emotions and spontaneous behaviour. Your Adult Role collects and organizes information, predicts the consequences of various actions and makes conscious decisions. Each role is equally valid. Using your Adult Role to think, plan and decide can increase your potential for success. But where would you be without the humour and flashes of inspiration provided by your Child Role?

And you need the caring and protection as well as the education which comes from the Parent. We must preserve all sides of ourselves to create a rounded personality.

ROLE PLAY

Have you ever had the following kind of conversation with yourself?

> I should go in and tell my boss that this project will not be ready on time. The photographs are delayed in the labs and the statistics are in the post. But he's been so irritable lately that I'm nervous about telling him. He'll probably be even angrier on hearing this news so I'll wait till next week.

This is a dialogue between your three personality parts. Your Parent Role – 'I should tell my boss' – is telling you what you *ought* to do. 'The project won't be ready, the photos are delayed, so are the stats' is your Adult Role, analysing and logical. The rest of the conversation is the Adapted Child fearing the reaction of the Parent. It can be useful to recognize the role-playing which unconsciously influences our decisions, helping or hindering our progress at work.

Roles can be especially helpful in protecting ourselves against aggression. I will give a few examples, but I am sure you will be able to think of many more which are particularly relevant to you.

- I recently met an enterprising woman who had started a cottage-letting business in the north-east. The business is very successful but, as can always happen, mistakes occur, cleaners let you down, slates fall off and damp gets in. On one occasion a client was very dissatisfied with the holiday home she had arrived at with such expectation. She was embarrassed in front of her friends and, encouraged by them, 'filled with righteous anger'. She stormed off to the Lettings Office to be met by the typist who was managing during the lunchbreak. She reeled off a string of complaints. The typist looked up and said petulantly, 'Well, you should've looked at the brochure properly, shouldn't you? We can't help the weather, it's been raining for weeks.' Here a Child was speaking to a Child and voices became raised, resulting in the keys being flung down so that they bounced on a filing tray and cut the typist's eye. The scene might have been quite different if the person on the front line, in this case the typist taking the brunt of the complaint for her absent boss, had been trained to react with her Parent and Adult Roles in this kind of situation. 'There does seem to be a problem here. Do sit down so I can make a note of it and then we can see what can be done. Perhaps you can give me all the details.' Here the Nurturing Parent is talking to the Child and then progressing to the Adult talking to the Adult. In this way aggression is defused and the facts assessed.

- A common scene of aggression is one where the Housing Officer calls at a highrise flat demanding rent or enquiring about a noise complaint. The occupants may not only be out of work but also 'moonlighting'; they may lack the communication skills to talk their way out of such a situation. In this case they may draw on the behaviour which served them well as a child: rebellious, threatening and physical. If the Housing Officer tackles the situation with an authoritarian Parental Role, the Child Role of the occupant may feel justified and its attempts be redoubled. Somehow lines of true communication need to be established between the two parties. The Housing Officer can ask for the help and cooperation of the occupant and between them they can discuss ways of settling the bill or curtailing the noise. Talking Adult to Adult can produce a rational, logical conversation and interaction at a level where both parties understand.

The manipulative wiles which may be exhibited in the Child Role occasionally raise the aggression level in others. I have watched, usually with amusement but also with a slight tinge of horror, as interviewers have 'assumed' behaviours with me over the past months in the hope that I will be conned by their subtly agreeing nods and 'sympathetic' eye contact to 'bare my soul' to the press (or whoever they happen to be). Behaviours that are donned like a mantle and are not based in reality – as contrasted to the Roles above, which are components of the personality – can easily provoke aggression. It was fortunate for us all that I, too, understood the game and could use my tension control techniques when I felt they had overstepped the mark. I also used my Adult Role to keep the conversation to 'facts', my Child Role to infuse a little humour and occasionally my Parental Role to draw the interview to a close or withhold an answer. It proved an essential technique for retaining my sanity!

CHAPTER 3

Assertiveness

Consultant:

MEG BOND
Assistant Director, Human Potential Research Project, University of
Surrey

All passages indicated by marginal arrows are directly derived from
Meg Bond, 'Being Assertive', Workbook and Reader for the Distance
Learning Centre, Polytechnic of the South Bank, London, 1987,
except where otherwise indicated.

I tried to analyse in retrospect why I had such a 'thing' about the concept of Assertiveness. The problem was solved for me when I was discussing with an eminent journalist the whole concept of the Suzy Lamplugh Trust and my enthusiasm for Assertiveness Training in particular. 'The trouble is,' he said, 'all the wrong people seem to go in for it.' It was then that it clicked. Everyone I have ever known well who took the courses either appeared very aggressive in the first place and became even more so, or else was so afraid to say boo to a mouse that any new communication technique either stumbled out or appeared manipulative.

Looking into it further, I realized that of course I had been blinkered in my approach and was only seeing the most obvious ends of the spectrum. The more I learn the more I realize that Assertiveness Training is a sensible communication technique from which everyone can benefit. Once again, I cannot imagine why it is not a standard part of induction courses at work, or even of the school curriculum.

To help me learn to use this valuable communication tool without raising or feeling aggression, I called on Meg Bond, Assistant Director of the Human Potential Research Project at the University of Surrey. Meg taught me that asserting yourself, or asserting your rights, is part of good clear communication. Asserting yourself means first working out what you want, then saying it clearly and negotiating with others. If you are assertive you retain your dignity and leave others the chance to retain theirs. Meg assured me that assertion does not mean being pushy, selfish or manipulative. You are more likely to be like this if you adopt a hostile approach which assumes that no compromise is possible. The only gains then will be those won by force. Blame, anger and making others feel guilty are the weapons used.

Assertiveness is based on the notion that everyone has certain rights as an individual person, whatever role they have in life. You yourself are a unique human being. Likewise, whatever you expect of other people because of their roles, they too are unique human beings with the same rights as everyone else. With these rights come responsibilities. You are responsible for yourself as a person, and no one should be allowed to take this responsibility away from you. Others are responsible for themselves, and you should not try to take this responsibility away or be manipulated into shouldering it.

1 Definition

Assertiveness is about respecting both our own and other people's rights, about taking responsibility for ourselves and helping other people to do likewise. How do we start to train ourselves, and how does it work in practice? Just as with TA, I needed help to answer this. The course I have followed in this chapter is entirely based on the course constructed by Meg Bond for the Distance Learning Centre of the Polytechnic of the South Bank. I am, or rather I was, a complete novice; naturally, a mere learner would have been incompetent to guide you through this exciting and rewarding experience.

To ensure we are all on the same wavelength, here is Meg Bond's definition of assertiveness: it is an approach to communicating with people in which self-respect and respect for other people are demonstrated. It involves:

- standing up for your own rights as a person and for those of others.
- making your own decisions for yourself and allowing others to do likewise.
- taking responsibility for your own feelings, opinions and actions and allowing others to do likewise.
- making your viewpoint and/or feelings known when you decide it is appropriate and allowing others to do likewise.
- letting others know what you want/need and allowing them to do likewise.
- setting your own limits (for example, by saying 'No') and allowing others to do likewise.
- giving compliments when they are due and accepting valid compliments.
- giving constructive criticism when it is due and accepting valid criticism of yourself, rejecting non-valid criticism.
- standing firm, compromising or cooperating according to your own assessment of what is appropriate to the situation, and allowing others to do likewise.

Assertiveness is about respecting your own and other people's rights, but we must look more closely at what these rights are. There is an outline below of the main ones. The list is taken from Meg Bond's *Stress and Self-Awareness: A Guide for Nurses* (1986) and is adapted from Anne Dickson's book on assertiveness, *A Woman in Your Own Right* (1982). These rights are expressed in both the first person and the second person, in order to emphasize the two sides of assertiveness: respecting one's own *and* other people's rights.

2 Assertive rights

1 I have the right to state my own needs and set my own priorities as a person, whatever other people expect of me because of my roles in life.

and

You have the right to state your own needs and set your own priorities as a person, whatever other people expect of you because of your roles in life.

2 I have the right to be treated with respect as an intelligent, capable and equal human being.

and

You have the right to be treated with respect as an intelligent, capable and equal human being.

3 I have the right to express my feelings.

and

You have the right to express your feelings.

4 I have the right to express my opinions and values.

and

You have the right to express your opinions and values.

5 I have the right to say yes or no for myself.

and

You have the right to say yes or no for yourself.

6 I have the right to make mistakes.

and

You have the right to make mistakes.

7 I have the right to change my mind.

and

You have the right to change your mind.

8 I have the right to say 'I don't understand.'

and

You have the right to say 'I don't understand.'

9 I have the right to ask for what I want.

and

You have the right to ask for what you want.

10 I have the right to decide for myself whether or not I am responsible for finding a solution to another person's problem.

and

You have the right to decide for yourself whether or not you are responsible for finding a solution to another person's problem.

11 I have the right to deal with *and* You have the right to deal
people without having to with people without having
make them like or approve to make them like or
of me. approve of you.

Let us take these rights one by one:

1 I have the right to state my own needs and set my own
priorities as a *person* whatever other people expect of me
because of my roles in life.

and

You have the right to state your own needs and set your own
priorities as a *person* whatever other people expect of you
because of your roles in life.

This assertive right means that although, for example, people at work
might always expect you to work late, change your day off at short
notice or cope with insufficient help, you have the right to decide to
put yourself and your own health first. You can set a limit to the
amount of effort you are prepared to put into helping out over and
above your basic job requirements. Remember that this is not being
selfish. In the long run everyone will benefit: you are less likely to be
exhausted and therefore you will be better and safer at your job, less
likely to become a workaholic and then have to stay off work through
illness.

Along with this right comes everyone's responsibility to decide for
themselves what their own needs and priorities are, and not to expect
others somehow to guess them or take them into account without
having been told. When we have not had the chance to learn
assertiveness it is quite common to get into the habit of expecting other
people to guess our needs, or understand them just from our hints. Or
we might just let others speak for us. Then we may resent it if they get
us wrong and our needs or priorities are not taken into account.

So we have the responsibility for deciding what is best for us and
speaking up for ourselves, and for letting other people do likewise.

When you have read this 'right' (I needed to re-read it in order to
absorb the meaning fully) take a few moments off to ponder on what it
means to you.

Two recent problems come to my mind. I teach swimming to
disabled and elderly adults for the Richmond Adult and Community

College. The college insisted that I enrol these classes at the pool the week before the beginning of term. This was, I felt, beyond my brief and a very difficult personal pressure, as I would have to deal with the paperwork and take in the money, limit the numbers and turn away many deserving cases. I asked the college to arrange for an RACC official to substitute for me but it was only when I 'asserted my rights' that they agreed. The results are that the students are satisfied that they have a fair chance, I am able to face the new class with a clear conscience, and the college have the classes they require.

Second, I recognize myself as a person who expects those who work with me to follow my thoughts by guesswork. I then find myself irritated and annoyed by their lack of intuition. This is an area I definitely need to work on.

Conversely, this right means that you and I have to allow others to set their own limits according to their own personal priorities. We cannot demand that they always go along with what we expect of them. This applies to customers and clients as well.

2　I have the right to be treated with respect as an intelligent, capable and equal human being.

and

You have the right to be treated with respect as an intelligent, capable and equal human being.

Many of us underestimate our own intelligence and capabilities. We might become used to feeling second-rate in the intelligence stakes, and when faced with someone who has had a more academic training, or who is higher up in the hierarchy, our own intelligence may be undervalued; we may allow others to ignore our contribution or opinions or to patronize us. Someone who allows people to treat them like this is likely to find themselves treating other people over whom they have seniority in exactly the same way.

So we have the responsibility to demonstrate that we wish to be treated as intelligent, capable and equal human beings and to treat others likewise. Again, it involves thinking and speaking for ourselves and allowing others to do so too.

Once again take time off to think about this 'right'.

We have in our family had to face it fairly and squarely. Having four dyslexic children, with my husband and me suffering to some degree from the problem, we know at first hand the difficulties in applying for jobs and attempting to progress without the letters or pieces of paper which proclaim our value on our behalf. It takes great self-confidence to know and be sure of your own worth with no outside body standing behind you. We have found it essential to be honest with ourselves when assessing our own value, and then to be convinced enough to be assured of our capabilities.

To be even more honest, as a family we still strive to join the 'norm'. I struggled through my Cert. Ed. FE & AE and I am inordinately proud of that certificate. Our son is now at university, having started at the age of twenty-seven. He worked night and day at his A-levels to get there. Obviously, we are still not quite confident or accepted enough to do without those pieces of paper which prove our worth.

However, because we all have had to do this consciously we may well be more understanding when it comes to other people under-valuing themselves. There are many situations in the workplace when employees hold an immense amount of 'power' over customers or clients. It is essential to establish a balance and understanding if aggression is to be defused or avoided. Everyone has a right to be treated with respect.

3 I have the right to express my feelings.
and
You have the right to express your feelings.

In this context, Meg was using the word 'feelings' to mean emotions as opposed to opinions or thoughts. The climate in the workplace tends strongly to discourage us from expressing emotions. This is probably because few of us have had the chance to learn how to express them assertively, so we end up making a mess of it, perhaps allowing them to get bottled up and then because of a 'last straw' over-reacting in a vicious outburst. Or perhaps we fall apart at a time when people are relying on us to get on with the job in hand.

It is important that we give ourselves – and everybody else – the opportunity to express feelings, particularly when we are involved in emotionally stressful events. This does not mean 'letting it all hang out' all the time and ignoring other responsibilities, but making the space and time for emotional expression. Time invested in letting off steam is time saved for the future: staff will be able to get back to concentrating on the job much more quickly.

It is assertive to take responsibility for our own feelings and not blame them on other people. Likewise, it is assertive to take responsibility for our own *actions*, but not for the emotions these actions may stimulate in someone else. For instance, if a colleague continues to hang around chatting when you have already explained to her that you want to get on with your work, your feelings of irritation are your responsibility. If you tell her that she is 'making you cross' then you are not taking responsibility for your own feelings. However, her actions are her responsibility. So, 'I feel cross when you continue to hang around chatting' is more assertive than 'You make me cross when you hang around chatting'. The first statement shows acceptance of responsibility for your own emotions.

On the other side of the coin, we are not responsible for other people's emotions. It is very common for someone to be blamed when a person is upset: 'Now look what you've done.' If you have been that person who has been blamed in the past, then you may continue to blame yourself when another person is upset.

For instance, if you are pointing out a mistake to someone at work and she bursts into tears, you are not responsible for her emotions. You are only responsible for your actions, in this case the way you put across your criticism. Perhaps you should have done it more tactfully or constructively. Perhaps not. Many of us are very sensitive to any kind of criticism, however tactful and constructive it is. We may have been heavily criticized in a destructive way in the past and any criticism in the present tends to revive those old feelings of hurt and humiliation. You are not responsible for these feelings in others.

This is a difficult one. Think about the last time you expressed your feelings at work. Did anyone support you? How did it turn out in the end? This does need some practice and careful thought. But it is important.

Assertiveness can give you the power to say 'I need help', or 'I am unhappy about this' when you are faced with worrying situations. Many employees have problems getting managers to accept that asking for help is a sign of professional competence, not professional failure.

The summer after Suzy disappeared, almost to the day, a similar incident happened: an accountant left his office, his coat with all his personal identification such as credit cards, chequebook and wallet still hanging on the back of his chair. He vanished into the afternoon in his shirtsleeves with £100 in his pocket which he had drawn from the bank that morning. However, this disappearance was not the same as Suzy's. The pressure in the workplace had been enormous and increasing, while he worked long dedicated hours, uncomplaining but sleepless at night because of the stress. His father died and he continued to bear up under the strain, refusing to 'take his problems to the office' but racked with guilt because he felt he had neglected his family commitments. One day he made a small mistake, the senior partner reprimanded him; he said not a word but simply walked out. His wife, children and office were all losers and so was the broken man suffering from 'burnout' who caught a train not knowing who he was or why or where he was going. In this case keeping his emotions to himself finally proved too much.

4 I have the right to express my opinions and values.
and
You have the right to express your opinions and values.

Whether or not we have a lot of knowledge or experience related to the topic under discussion, we do have the right to have an opinion and to express that opinion. Our opinions can be very valuable.

This applies to other people: whether or not they have what we would consider to be appropriate knowledge or expertise, they still have the right to an opinion and to express it. Opinions are rarely absolutely right or wrong. They are merely the points of view of the individuals expressing them.

Along with our right to have an opinion and to express it, we also have the responsibility of acknowledging our opinions as our own. Making generalizations or pretending to speak for a number of people may indicate that we are not taking responsibility for our own opinions or values. Speaking in the first person – that is, 'I think . . .' rather than 'We think . . .' – helps us to express our opinions assertively.

Listen to yourself speaking. I have found it necessary to correct myself from hiding behind 'we', and have also made a conscious effort to 'get my thoughts together'. I find it far too easy to be long-winded and go off the point.

5 I have the right to say yes or no for myself.
and
You have the right to say yes or no for yourself.

This right is closely connected to the first one. Whatever we consider our own priorities to be, we have the right to make our own decisions about whether to accept or turn down a request from someone else.

Many of us are conditioned into doing what other people want, and do not consider our own wishes. But we have the right to decide for ourselves whether to agree or not. Similarly other people have the right to decide for themselves whether to go along with any requests we make of them or to refuse. We need to bear this in mind when making requests of people: they have the right to turn us down.

Our responsibility in this respect is, first, in making our own decisions and taking responsibility for them even if in retrospect they turn out to be the wrong ones. Second, it is our responsibility to allow other people to make their own decisions, and not impede or interfere with their right to do so.

It has taken me years to learn when to say no and to decline with ease and without regrets. I also used to find it a temptation to answer for those who I felt could not speak up for themselves. Working on Sport for the Visually Handicapped for the Disabled Living Foundation certainly gave me the right perspective. These students left me in no doubt that they could and would make their own decisions even if it did mean bumping into a door. I was left with a profound respect which has grown through the years as I have become involved with people with many different disabilities.

6 I have the right to make mistakes.
and
You have the right to make mistakes.

This right does not give us a charter for carelessness, but it does acknowledge that every human being makes mistakes. The expectation that anyone should be perfect and should be able to do anything and everything perfectly, whatever the conditions, is totally unrealistic. If we expect this of ourselves and then are devastated when we make a mistake, we will put ourselves in a despairing state of mind which will make it difficult to learn from the mistake.

If we over-react to others' mistakes, perhaps by wielding the disciplinary procedure unnecessarily, we will make it more difficult for them to learn and therefore to prevent the mistake recurring.

It is important to acknowledge our own mistakes and to be able to point out gently to other people the mistakes they make, without making a big fuss about it. To deny mistakes is unhelpful; we can learn from them. Think back over your life, especially at work. Outline to yourself what you have learned from the mistakes you have made during your career. Try this one out on your colleagues too, and try to persuade them to share their examples. It will probably be a relief to find you are not the only one who makes mistakes. It certainly helped me to be able to acknowledge this both to myself and to others.

7 I have the right to change my mind.
and
You have the right to change your mind.

Mistakes can include decisions which, after further thought, we realize are the wrong decisions. Apart from that, it is only natural in the course of time to change opinions and values in the light of further experience and knowledge. Unless our minds become fossilized it is impossible to stay consistent all the time.

As far as dealing with other people is concerned, it is important to avoid the pitfall of seeking false security by expecting other people to be consistent all the time. Our responsibilities with regard to this right tie in with the responsibilities for making our own decisions and for our own opinions, which include being willing to change our minds in the light of further information or experience. As the saying goes, 'The mind is like a parachute: it functions only when open.'

Working in the field of movement and exercise has ensured that with so many approaches, concepts and ideas arising from new research, we have in the British Slimnastics Association had to build into our training manuals room for changes of mind. There always has to be space for updating, improvement and expansion. This must be the case in our own lives too. But keeping an open mind takes energy and a youthful outlook – it helps to be fit. When discussing safety procedures with the management of various organizations, I have sometimes been saddened by the closed minds and I'm-all-right-Jack attitudes I have met. Anyone who can categorically state that they have a near-perfect system for their staff is verging on the complacent. In teaching we are always taught to evaluate ourselves, our methods and results on a constant and regular basis.

8 I have the right to say 'I don't understand.'
and
You have the right to say 'I don't understand.'

No single person can be expected to know everything or understand everything that is explained to them (especially if it's explained badly). So, however supercilious or sarcastic someone is when you admit to not understanding something, remember you have the right to say that you do not understand. In fact, you have a *responsibility* to admit you do not understand if faced with some aspect of your work for which you have had insufficient training. Likewise, you have the responsibility for allowing others to admit that they do not understand without putting them down. Whatever our expectations are of a person, or however long it takes someone to grasp what we are trying to explain, they have the right not to understand.

Communication is a two-way process. We must use appropriate vocabulary and ideas if we want to be understood, rather than showing off our knowledge or 'in-crowd-ness' by using unintelligible jargon or abbreviations.

Jargon is my pet hate. But I have had to realize that what is jargon to me is another man's normal language. Looking back on the time when I worked at the BBC I remember we used to converse in initials: 'I need the ETA for the CP Tel with the DDP' (the estimated time of arrival for the Controller of Programmes, Television with the Deputy Director of Programmes). It must have been impossible for those outside to translate but it was easily intelligible to us. I now do not hesitate to ask for explanations, otherwise I can spend hours in meetings with my mind wandering through a fog, waiting hopefully for a picture to appear. Hiding behind jargon can build up aggression or lower into depression the person on the receiving end if they are not fully in the know. If you are not within a particular trade union, for instance, you can listen to the rules, sub-clauses, numbers and dates and feel most insecure, finding no opening through which you can communicate. Doctors can reduce a patient to the status of the third-form admissions group by reeling off a condition, its treatment and possible side-effects in jargon that is matched by the prescription and the notes, which are carefully hidden. Frustration can easily set in!

9 I have the right to ask for what I want.

and

You have the right to ask for what you want.

We may not always have the right to *get* what we want, but we certainly have the right to ask for it. On the other side of the coin, when someone asks us for something we do not always have to comply: we can decide for ourselves.

Asking for what you want does not have to be something very big, or a demand. Just asking someone to give you the time is an assertive request. You probably frequently make assertive requests without noticing, but in a stressful situation it becomes more difficult to know what you want and how to say it.

Your responsibilities in this respect include working out what you want and letting the relevant people know, rather than expecting them to guess. Similarly, you need to be willing to allow other people opportunities to express their wishes and to respect their right to ask for what they want.

One day at work, consciously notice the times you ask someone to do something. Jot down the actual words you used and then analyse how clearly you made your request. It may prove quite an eye opener.

10   I have the right to decide for myself whether or not I am responsible for finding a solution to another person's problem.

and

You have the right to decide for yourself whether or not you are responsible for finding a solution to another person's problem.

When faced with someone who has a problem, we often feel obliged to find a solution, either by doing something practical or by giving advice. There is often a feeling of guilt if no solution can be offered. It is up to us to decide whether we have a responsibility for finding a solution to a problem.

Other people have that right too. They may decide that they are not responsible for finding a solution to *our* problem, and put that responsibility back on to us. This right speaks for itself. It is so hard not to jump in and help people, especially if we feel we can. It is going to take some time for me to learn to hold back and not immediately offer all the 'good' advice that I instinctively want to pour forth.

11   I have the right to deal with people without having to make them like or approve of me.

and

You have the right to deal with people without having to make them like or approve of you.

Everyone needs to be liked to some extent, but sometimes the desire to be liked can lead us into becoming submissive or manipulative. It is not always possible for us to like or approve of each other. Out of this arises a lot of behind-the-scenes backbiting which is not good for any relationship. It is healthier to get things out into the open, deal with misunderstandings and clarify values and boundaries.

It is not essential to our effectiveness to be liked by all our colleagues and those we work for all the time. It is not even possible!

Likewise, when colleagues disagree with us, stand up to us or even offend us, we may not like them. We do not have to like them all the time to be effective. Neither do they have to bend over backwards to make us like them.

Think for a moment whether this right affects you. Nearly all of us can pinpoint situations when the desire to be liked gets in the way of being assertive.

When you face a totally awful situation, as my family and I have done, it strips away the unnecessary hang-ups in your character. Looking back, I am sure I often acted or made decisions simply hoping to please and then regretted my move. I now realize that life is too short and too precious to squander. I do not think this has made me insensitive to the needs and wishes of others, but I do not waste time wondering if my actions will be popular. It has been an incredible freedom.

3 Assertive and non-assertive approaches

In this section Meg asks us to look at a framework describing four ways of dealing with people:

- aggressive
- submissive/passive
- manipulative and, of course,
- assertive

You will have the opportunity to consider the main features of each approach, some possible reasons for each being used, and some common reactions to them from others. Each of these four approaches can be considered with regard to the amount of respect demonstrated both for your own assertive rights and for the other person's assertive rights.

AGGRESSIVE

Meg's course showed me that the aggressive approach demonstrates respect for our own rights, but not for those of the other person. You will come over as aggressive if you:

- make other people's decisions for them.
- make your own decisions without taking into consideration the views and priorities of the people who will be affected by those decisions.
- give orders when a request would be more appropriate, in order not to give the other person a chance to reply.
- insist that your opinion is right and put other people down for holding a different viewpoint.
- interrupt a lot when the other person is talking.
- are pushy, bulldozing someone to do something against their wishes.
- make threats.
- attack or criticize the other person's personality or use put-downs.
- are overly critical, not acknowledging people's good points too.
- find someone else to blame when something goes wrong.
- retaliate when you feel threatened.
- refuse to acknowledge your own mistakes and faults.
- pick at the other person's vulnerable points.
- are competitive, trying to prove your superiority over the other person.
- use verbal or physical abuse.
- angrily over-react.
- argue or create conflict for the sake of it.

Aggressive body language

Often it is not so much a matter of *what* is said, but *how* it is said. Sometimes the words that are spoken can be perfectly assertive, but the body language that goes with them conveys aggression. For example:

- *Posture:* may be tense and erect, with an attempt to get physically higher than the other person, perhaps standing while they are sitting.

- *Gestures:* tense, strong gestures with the hands closed can be interpreted as aggressive, such as chopping movements with the hands, clenched fists, the index finger pointed or waving and poking, hands on hips, tapping or shuffling feet.

- *Eye contact:* may be hard, glaring or staring, perhaps from a higher position than the other person.

- *Facial expression:* may be tense, with frowns, gritted teeth, pursed lips, an angry smile or narrowed eyes. The expression may display a high strength of feeling inappropriate to the situation.

- *Voice:* may be sharp, threatening and generally stronger than is necessary.

- *Distance:* may be uncomfortably close at times, or far enough away to make it difficult for the other person to respond. Aggressive behaviour also includes walking away before the other person has had a chance to respond.

Why be aggressive?

It is often assumed that people who behave in an aggressive way are just naturally like that. However, there are several reasons why people's approaches might be aggressive at times. You might recognize some of them in yourself as well as in others.

- *Lack of confidence:* Under stress it is easy to lose confidence in yourself and perhaps to try to hide this by being aggressive. Someone who is habitually aggressive most of the time is likely to have a very low opinion of themselves underneath it all.

- *Anxiety:* This may lead someone to want to be in control of everything and everyone. For instance, newly qualified managers are sometimes quite aggressive in their approach while they go through the anxious first few months in their new role.

- *Aggressive role models:* A person may get the impression from aggressive seniors that they should behave in the same way when they gain a senior post. A man may have been conditioned to think that aggression and competition are part of being a man.

- *Bottled-up anger:* The climate in the workplace does not make it easy to show anger appropriately and therefore it often gets bottled up over a period of time. This causes over-reactions. Someone who has been submissive for a while will have a backlog of repressed resentments so that, when she finally tries to stand up for herself, it may come out too strongly in an aggressive approach.

- *'Knock-on' effect down the hierarchy:* If you are on the receiving end of aggressive approaches from further up the hierarchy and find it difficult to respond assertively, you may well display your frustrations in an aggressive way with people junior to you.

- *Lack of opportunity to learn assertiveness:* You may just not know what to do or say and slip into aggressive habits.

- *Short-term gains:* Only taking into account short-term gains such as getting particular jobs done, saving time or reducing your own immediate pressures, rather than thinking about the long-term effects on your relationship with the other person, may well come across as aggressive – and probably won't help to deal with the source of the problem.

Reactions to aggression

People's reactions when they are confronted with aggressive behaviour vary widely, often because of their previous experiences with aggression. Reactions may, for example, include:

- *Reciprocal aggression:* the person on the receiving end may immediately fight back in a like manner.

- *Submissive defeat:* they may give in against their will and harbour increasing resentment against the aggressive person.

- *Indirect aggression* or manipulation: the victim may not retaliate directly but may get back in less obvious ways, perhaps by not cooperating at a later date or by sabotaging from behind the scenes.

- *Inability to take in valid points:* the aggressive approach may put people's backs up so much that they are unable to grasp any valid points which are being made; they may dismiss everything being said because the manner in which it is said is inappropriate.

- *Avoidance:* persistent aggressiveness may lead some people to avoid you because you are too tiring to have around.

- *Getting trapped into interpersonal 'games'* (See Eric Berne's book *Games People Play*, 1967): if you use an aggressive approach with the same person a few times, you may find them responding in such a way that you get caught in a 'script', almost like a scene from a play, in which you are always the bossy, oppressive one. This can become a habit that is hard to break, even when you deliberately try to do so.

SUBMISSIVE

When we are being submissive, we are not showing respect for our own assertive rights nor taking responsibility for ourselves. You will come over as submissive when you:

- allow other people to make your decisions.
- make decisions without taking yourself, your own needs, wants, priorities, opinions and values into account.
- hold back from saying what you want, or make a request with an inappropriately low strength of feeling so the other person does not realize how important it is to you.
- give up at the first hurdle, even if something is important to you.
- say yes when you would really rather say no.
- allow yourself to be persuaded or bulldozed into something against your will.
- allow yourself to be interrupted a lot.
- do most of the listening in an ordinary conversation (although a counselling-type conversation is different – your role then is to do most of the listening).
- allow other people to attack you and put you down as a person.
- complain behind the scenes about not getting what you want or about being the victim of unfairness and injustice, without going to the person directly involved.
- put yourself down or refuse compliments.
- wait for something good to happen to you without making any attempt to set it in motion yourself.
- wait for someone else to guess what you want and give it to you.
- avoid confrontation at all costs, smoothing things over when they really need to be aired or dealt with.
- under-react by not showing justifiable anger or not showing your true strength of feeling about something.
- fail to set limits and let the other person walk all over you, perhaps bringing out the bully in even the nicest person.

Submissive body language
As with the aggressive approach, a submissive response is often demonstrated by body language. For instance:

- *Posture:* may be slumped and defeated or tense and agitated. It may include allowing yourself to be towered over.

- *Gestures:* may include nervous movements such as fiddling, touching the face a lot, covering the mouth while speaking or pulling the elbows and knees in. Alternatively there may be a kind of paralysis with no gestures at all.

- *Eye contact:* may be poor, avoiding the other person's eyes. Or it may be good eye contact, showing too much willingness to listen.

- *Facial expression:* may show defeat and tension or a desire to placate with pleading smiles or an over-apologetic look.

- *Voice:* may be inappropriately quiet, tentative, hesitant, shrill or obsequious; the tone of voice may be rather childlike or sound defeated.

- *Distance:* may include allowing the other person to come uncomfortably close or to remain at a distance at which it is difficult for you to respond easily.

Why be submissive?

The reasons why people are sometimes or even habitually submissive are in some ways similar to those for being aggressive, although of course the result is different.

- *Lack of confidence:* Stress may lead you to lose self-respect and slide into being submissive.

- *Anxiety:* Under threat (real or imagined) you may go into 'freeze' or 'flight' responses and so end up using a submissive approach. On the other hand if you *choose* to 'fly' you may be taking an assertive action.

- *Submissive role models:* You may have picked up the notion that to be a 'nice person' (or 'feminine') you have to put everyone else first all the time and never take yourself into account. Perhaps the people you looked up to in the past were like this, or told you to be.

- *Bottled-up anger:* This can also lead to being submissive. You may feel so frustrated about something that you dare not say anything in case you blow your top.

- *Lack of opportunity to learn assertiveness:* You may just not know what to do or say and slip into submissive habits in spite of the wish to be assertive.

- *Short-term gains:* You might find yourself only taking immediate gains into consideration, such as keeping the peace, being liked or reducing immediate stress, rather than thinking about the long-term effects.

Reactions to submissiveness
Submissive behaviour inevitably provokes reactions from other people, usually negative ones. These may include:

- *Lack of consideration:* this may be intentional or unintentional. If it is intentional, the other person may be delighted that you go along with him and plough on in his own way. On the other hand, he may prefer that you say your bit but, since you do not, assume that everything is okay with you.

- *'Flogging a willing horse':* having been submissive once or twice before, you may be seen as an easy touch and get more and more demands on your time and energy as a result.

- *Bullying:* persistent submissiveness may result in the other person becoming irritated and impatient. This can lead even the nicest of people to become bullies. You may attract bullying types to you.

- *Avoidance:* persistent submissiveness may result in some people avoiding you because you are too irritating to have around.

- *Getting trapped in interpersonal 'games':* as with the aggressive approach, habits can be built up which are difficult to break. If you have been submissive with someone a few times, they may react in such a way as to set up a scene, as if from a play, in which each of you acts out a part in the script: you could become the 'victim' or 'martyr'.

MANIPULATIVE

The manipulative approach is a sort of indirect aggression: it appears to acknowledge and respect the other person's rights, but in the end does not really do so at all. You will come over as manipulative when you:

- make other people's decisions for them in such a way that initially they think they have decided for themselves.
- make your own decisions while appearing to take into account the views and priorities of the other people involved, but in fact only paying lip service to the idea of consultation.

- use insincere ego-boosting to get what you want.
- try to convince others that they really want or think exactly what you would prefer.
- try to make others feel guilty.
- opt out of something by forgetting it or citing excuses without a clear refusal.
- make veiled threats, hinting at unpleasant consequences.
- give the impression that you are speaking on behalf of a number of other people when you are really just expressing your own personal point of view or preference.
- drop hints and expect others to know exactly what you mean and then get resentful when they misunderstand.
- try to sidetrack someone away from something you want to avoid dealing with.
- say one thing to a person's face but say or do the opposite behind his back.
- praise or explain something to someone in a patronizing way.
- are sarcastic or make put-downs in a jokey way (smiling demolition).
- put the blame for your own mistakes or faults on to other people.
- talk your way out of a situation where you are being justly criticized.
- use flirtation to get your own way.
- appear to listen, while not really listening at all.
- interrupt when others are having their way, perhaps pretending you know exactly what they mean or what they were going to say.
- put words into other people's mouths.
- are over-friendly or ultra-charming to get what you want.
- put someone down by categorizing their personality according to some theory or other, in the guise of being 'objective' or 'caring'.
- get at someone behind the scenes by criticizing them behind their back, or sabotaging their efforts by persuading other people to lose motivation or opt out of some scheme.

Manipulative body language

In the same way that a person's body language can indicate an aggressive or submissive approach, a manipulative impression can be conveyed non-verbally. For example:

- *Posture:* may be over-relaxed, over-friendly, coy, flirtatious, exaggeratedly elegant or very laid-back. There may be a hint of aggression, perhaps if you arrange yourself to be at a higher level than the other person.

- *Gestures:* may be exaggerated in terms of friendliness, elegance, flirtatiousness and so on. There may be signs of indirect aggression, including hand-crunching or over-hard jocular slaps on the back. There may be patronizing touching or patting.

- *Eye contact:* may include looking out of the tops or the sides of the eyes or avoiding eye contact at crucial moments, but may also be direct.

- *Facial expression:* may be exaggeratedly friendly, innocent or concerned, appearing to be listening very well.

- *Voice:* may be exaggerated in its gentleness or friendliness, perhaps with a pleading or flirtatious note. There may be a tone of veiled threat, with underlying criticism or sarcasm.

- *Distance:* may be too close for comfort, as part of the exaggerated friendliness, or may be too distant for the other person to make a response easily.

Why be manipulative?

As with the other approaches, people can sometimes find themselves being manipulative, particularly when things are difficult for them.

- *Lack of confidence:* Stress may lead you to want to boost your confidence by controlling people or putting them down, but this time in a more subtle manner than in the aggressive approach.

- *Anxiety:* The need to be in control of everyone around you, ensuring that they always believe or do things exactly as you want them to, can unconsciously arise from anxiety. The desire to be liked may lead you to do this in as nice and as charming a way as possible, so you end up being manipulative.

- *Manipulative role models:* You may have been taught by example that the manipulative approach is best.

- *Bottled-up anger:* This may lead you unconsciously to put people down by using a manipulative approach. Since it is indirect aggression you can deny any intention of aggression if confronted. For instance, the jokey put-down is often explained as, 'Only a joke; have you no sense of humour?'

- *Lack of opportunity to learn assertiveness:* Again, you may just not know how to be assertive and slip into manipulative behaviour in spite of good intentions.

- *Short-term gains:* The manipulative approach is very tempting if you are keen to get something done now. In the short term, it is probably the most effective way of getting what you want. However, the long-term results can damage a relationship through a lack of trust.

Reactions to manipulation

Responses to the manipulative approach can in the end damage relationships. You may find the result to be apparent immediate success; since the approach can be so effective in getting what you want in the short term, it can lead you to believe that it is the best way to deal with people. Ultimately, however, some of the following reactions are likely to occur:

- *Distrust:* if you are frequently manipulative with someone, they will come to realize what you are doing and mistrust your motives. On the occasions when you *are* being genuine, direct and honest, they will be unable to take you at face value and will instead wonder what you are up to.

- *Retaliation:* the people who realize that you are trying to manipulate them may retaliate aggressively or may later get back at you themselves in manipulative ways.

- *Avoidance:* people whom you have manipulated in the past may avoid you because you are too complicated to deal with.

- *Getting trapped into interpersonal 'games':* someone may react to your manipulation by playing the other part of the script so that you both get locked into a game. This becomes a habit and you then find it hard to break out of the game and relate to each other seriously, as two adult people. Flirtation is one example: you both get into the habit of flirting until you are sick of it, but then you find it difficult to stop.

ASSERTIVE

The assertive approach involves respecting your own rights and those of others, and taking responsibility for yourself and allowing others to do likewise. It does not guarantee that you will get what you want, but it is a 'Win–Win' situation in that both people are treated as equals and both are taken into consideration. It does not guarantee that the other person will always like you or be happy with your approach, but it does give them the opportunity to be taken seriously and to know where they stand with you.

Assertive body language
An assertive approach is reflected by more than the words that are spoken. Non-verbal communication is an important part of assertiveness. For example:

- *Posture:* usually relaxed, relatively calm, well balanced and upright, facing the other person at the same level and not moving unnecessarily.

- *Gestures:* generally relaxed but, if indicating the strength of feeling behind what is being said, with open hands and not invading the other person's space.

- *Eye contact:* direct but relaxed and at the same eye level as the other person, indicating a willingness to listen.

- *Facial expression:* generally relaxed, firm, open and pleasant, without inappropriate smiles, displaying suitable strength of feeling. Indicates a willingness to listen on equal terms.

- *Voice:* generally relaxed and low-pitched, with a firm gentle tone and enough volume to be heard clearly, though it may show an appropriate amount of emotion to indicate the strength of feeling behind what is being said.

- *Distance:* an average, comfortable proximity, making it easy for the other person to respond.

Why be assertive?
The assertive approach is the most positive of the four approaches, both for you and for the people with whom you come into contact. Being assertive can help you, both professionally and personally, in the following ways:

- *Regaining confidence:* Everyone gets stressed and has times when self-confidence goes. By deliberately using assertive methods you can help yourself deal with stress, keep your self-esteem from sinking and bolster your confidence when faced with a stressful situation. This does not mean that you become big-headed, but that you retain a balanced view of yourself. You can keep a realistic belief in yourself, your abilities, your value as a person and your rights, while acknowledging and accepting your faults and mistakes and trying to do something about them without punishing yourself.

- *Controlling anxiety:* Assertive methods can help you to accept that it is all right to be human and have emotions such as anxiety, and to prevent that anxiety from taking over.

- *Assertive role model:* By being assertive you can demonstrate to other people that there is an alternative to aggression, submission and being manipulative. You make it easier for others to be assertive as well. This is important if junior staff, colleagues and senior staff are to develop their own assertiveness.

- *Using anger constructively:* Assertive methods will help you to express anger appropriately and to use the energy of anger to get things done, rather than suppressing it and dumping it on people who don't deserve it.

- *Long-term gains:* Although plucking up the energy and courage to be assertive in difficult situations does cause increased short-term stress, in the long term you will have less stress and better working relationships (and personal ones too). You will be more effective in your work, whatever it is.

Reactions to assertiveness

Most of the time an assertive approach is quite straightforward, and so acceptance and easy communication are common reactions. You may be surprised at how often things go well when you are being assertive. People know where they stand with you, they are less likely to misunderstand you, so they can feel secure with you. This means there is less anxiety overall, and so less chance of non-assertive reactions.

On the other hand, you will probably encounter some non-assertive responses; some people find it hard to cope with an assertive approach at first and may persist in responding aggressively, submissively or in a manipulative way. However, if you have given them ample opportunity to respond assertively, their lack of assertiveness is not your responsibility. It may cause you problems, but then you would have had more problems with those people had you not been assertive. 'You can't win 'em all.' There is no formula for 100 per cent success in dealing with human beings, but the assertive approach will give you a higher percentage than the other three.

Try to recall the distinguishing features of the assertive approach. Try to think of as many as you can before referring back to the text to refresh your memory.

Now try to remember the assertive rights and responsibilities outlined in pages 63–73. Try to think of as many as you can before referring back to the text to refresh your memory.

When to be more assertive
As we work through the next three sections we will be constructing our own assertiveness training programme, concentrating on how to be successfully assertive by communicating more effectively. But first we have to identify more clearly *when* it is that we need to be assertive.

Many people have greater difficulty in being assertive when they feel stressed. Everyone experiences stress: we each have a 'crumple button' or 'Achilles' heel'. While you may be perfectly assertive in certain situations, others might make you lose confidence or forget about being assertive. The types of situation which affect each of us can vary widely from discussing an issue with someone (or in a group) who has strong feelings with which we disagree, listening to scathing comments about our opinions or the way we have expressed them, to saying no when someone makes an unreasonable demand or even saying no when someone makes a reasonable request with which we do not really want to comply, and then sticking to our decision under pressure or manipulation. There are many more examples we can probably think of in our working lives. Choose five problem situations of your own and think about how you could tackle them with an assertive approach.

4 Becoming more assertive

Now we have reached the point where Meg Bond looks at ways of expressing opinions, taking part in a balanced discussion and making requests. Getting our point across and allowing others to do so is a fundamental part of assertiveness. If a person's point of view, preferences and needs are to be taken into account, then they need to be made known. You will have the opportunity to compare the advantages of an assertive approach with non-assertive approaches, to notice which aspects of assertiveness come easily to you, and to see where you need to practise assertive techniques.

EXPRESSING OUR OPINIONS

First of all, we need to distinguish between the four main ways of expressing opinions, and look at the features of each one in turn.

Assertive approach
The main points of the assertive approach are to:

- remember you have a right to hold an opinion and to have it heard.
- make an opportunity to state your opinion, perhaps by eventually interrupting if the other person does not give you a chance to come in, or by arranging a time or a meeting with someone to put forward your opinion, or by putting it in writing.
- make a clear statement of your own opinion, speaking for yourself and preferably using the first person: i.e. 'I think . . .', 'It seems to me . . .', 'I get the impression . . .', In my opinion . . .'.
- if someone tries to interrupt you a lot, either ignore the interruption and continue to make your point or say, 'Let me just finish . . .' or words to that effect; then, when you have finished, make a point of asking them what they were going to say – and then listen.
- remember that other people have a right to their opinions too.
- give others a chance to state their opinions without interrupting them unless they go on and on at great length or interrupt you a lot.
- recognize that you may need to acknowledge disagreement and just leave it at that.
- pinpoint exactly where you *do* agree with someone. Even where there are strong disagreements, there is usually some common ground somewhere.
- remember that you will find all the above points more difficult to carry through if you are overstressed and tense. Unless you release the tension your judgment is likely to be impaired and your delivery hampered.
- remind yourself, too, that your attitudes matter. Non-verbal communication is equally essential when you are expressing your opinions or listening to others, especially when it may denote aggression.

Compare these points with the main features of the other three approaches:

Aggressive approach
- insisting on your right to have and express opinions but not allowing others the same right.
- insisting your own opinion is 'right' – and that's the end of it.
- not giving the other person a chance to reply to your opinion, perhaps by walking away or interrupting them a lot.
- putting other people's opinions down, for example: 'Don't be ridiculous . . .', 'That's stupid . . .', 'How on earth could you believe that. . . ?', 'Nonsense!'.
- expressing your opinions as though they were cut-and-dried facts, rather than matters of opinion.

Submissive approach
- not respecting your own right to have opinions.
- not bothering to form opinions on matters which affect your life.
- holding back, not expressing an opinion even when you have the opportunity.
- not making the opportunity to express opinions; for instance, not interrupting or not making arrangements to see somebody who needs to know your opinion.
- if you do express an opinion, doing so in an unconvincing way, perhaps too tentatively or without enough strength of feeling.
- allowing yourself to be interrupted and put down a lot.
- allowing yourself to be swayed by other people's strong opinions which are contrary to your own.
- seeking approval for your opinions.

Manipulative approach
- acknowledging your own right to have an opinion – but not the other person's.
- dressing up your opinion as an apparent 'fact' and putting it across in an apparently conciliatory way.
- generalizing and making your opinion look as though other people agree with you; for instance, 'We all know that . . . or 'We always think . . .'.
- trying to put your own words into the other person's mouth; for

instance, 'Don't you think that. . . ?' or 'I'm sure you'll agree with me when I say . . .'.

- setting it up so that the other person is in a bad light if they disagree with you, such as 'Any intelligent person can see that . . .'.
- appearing to listen to and understand the other person but in fact not doing so, perhaps interrupting.
- trying to talk the other person round to your point of view at all costs.
- making jokey or sarcastic put-downs of other people's opinions.
- pretending to show respect for a point of view when you don't really have it; for example, 'With respect . . .'.
- showing contempt with your body language while your words give an impression of respect.

ASSERTIVE DISCUSSION

We will now go on to look at the skills involved in taking part in a balanced discussion. But first, why do we need to be assertive in discussion?

The purpose

The purpose of discussion is to give the people involved the opportunity to:

- clarify their own point of view by having the chance to think aloud with the attention of someone else.
- listen to and be stimulated by other people's ideas, sparking off new links and new directions in thought.
- make the views of the participants known in order that they can be taken into account when decisions are being made.
- use the resources available by putting ideas together: 'two heads are better than one'.
- be listened to, and feel acknowledged and important as human beings and as part of a team.
- build relationships with one another.

If discussion is to fulfil these purposes, then everyone involved needs to have an equal opportunity to join in fully. Often there is a lack of balance in a discussion, with one person mostly listening and one person mostly talking. This can lead to problems on both sides. The good listener may feel taken for granted or unnoticed, or feel that the other person is not interested in her; the enthusiastic talker may wonder what the listener is thinking and resent her keeping her opinions and ideas to herself, leaving the talker to expose herself more by talking on.

Listening too much

If you cannot get a word in edgeways and end up doing most of the listening, you will have to interrupt to get a point across. The problem with this is that when the talker is in full swing, her thoughts may be going along their own train and she may not listen to your interruption. It can therefore be useful to give a lead – a phrase which gives her a chance to switch her attention to you. For example:

'Can I just say something here. . . ?'
'I'd just like to make a point here . . .'
'That reminds me of . . .'
'That makes me think of . . .'
'Going back to what you said earlier . . .'
'There's something I feel very strongly about on this topic . . .'

Eye contact, body language, all can be brought into play, so that despite your interruption the speaker can feel valued and any potential defensive aggression can be defused.

Asserting your opinion

When you express your opinion, you must not allow the other person to interrupt you until you have had a reasonable amount of time to have your say. You can prevent an interruption by just sticking to your point and ignoring it until you have finished. Or you could simply say 'Let me finish . . .'. Once more a smile, a gesture and your general attitude can indicate that you do not intend to dominate the floor but, on the other hand, you do need to get your point across. Control your tension level, too, or you may appear impatient and dogmatic.

Allowing a response

It is important to give the other person the chance to respond to what you have said, or, indeed, to get them to acknowledge that you have said it at all. You may need to ask an open question such as 'How do you see it?', 'What do you think?' or 'What were you going to say?' You may still have to break into the discussion a few more times in order to reassert your right to equal opportunity of expression. Most people eventually get the message that you want to take an equal part and want them to do their share of the listening. Unfortunately some people do not, however hard you try. If you want to continue the relationship, this can be raised as a problem (not a blame session) which needs to be tackled by both sides. Using the Transactional Analysis and falling into your Child Role in which you can use humour to release the tension in a situation is a very useful technique when used with discretion and good timing.

Talking too much

If you find yourself doing most of the talking in a discussion, you should try to find ways of holding back some of the things you want to say without actually stifling your enthusiasm, interest or strength of feeling.

Allowing a response

At the end of each of your main points, it is important to leave a silence so that the other person can think out what to say and get it said. Or you may need to ask an open question to find out their opinion. Some people find it difficult to bear silences; this might be your problem. If your mind races or you get physically agitated, you might do well to practise some relaxation techniques to slow yourself down a bit. When my mind starts to wander or rush on to something else, I try to put my attention back to what the other person is saying by repeatedly saying to myself silently, 'I'm listening, I'm listening, I'm listening.' I also try to make sure I am looking at the talker, without staring. As we have already seen, if you keep your eyes fixed you may momentarily cease to think and this can prove very embarrassing.

Summarizing

If you find yourself doing more than your share of interrupting and you find listening difficult, you might need to practise some listening techniques. Summarizing can help you to concentrate. Listen carefully to the opinions the other person is putting across and try to pick out the main points. When they have finished, summarize the key aspects of what they were saying very briefly and check with them to see if you've got it right.

Noticing body language

When you realize that you have been doing most of the talking try to notice body language which might tell you the other person is tired of listening. These signs will not always mean that someone is bored and does not care; it is just not humanly possible to listen for long periods. Most people can't concentrate for more than about three minutes or so before the brain switches off. Signs of tiredness and lack of attention may include fidgeting, slumping, looking as though they are about to move away or glancing at a watch. Try to draw your point to a close and give them a chance to speak.

MAKING REQUESTS ASSERTIVELY

Before you can use assertive skills to make requests, and before you can be ready to counter non-assertive responses to these requests, it is essential that you know exactly what you want.

Knowing what you want

The first step in asserting your own needs or preferences is *knowing* what they are. Many people find this fundamental step in assertiveness the most difficult, perhaps because many of us are trained to think about what 'ought', 'should' or 'must' be done, rather than considering what we actually want or need.

These shoulds, oughts and musts arise out of expectations from others which become fixed in our minds and interfere with our ability to listen to ourselves. An important part of caring is the ability to listen to other people, to listen to their wants and needs. This is also an essential part of assertiveness. But before a person can really be an effective listener to someone else, they need to be able to listen to themselves. This section may help you listen to yourself a little more.

Making positive statements

Often it is easier to pinpoint what we do *not* want. However, if we communicate this to other people, it can leave them in limbo; they do not necessarily have a clear picture of what we *do* want. In fact, the picture that is conjured up in their minds will be the exact opposite of what we want. For instance, if you hand a child or a confused adult a full cup of fluid and say 'Do not spill it,' the first thing they will sometimes do is spill it. This is because the picture you have conjured up in their minds is a negative one. If you can work out *exactly* what you want and communicate it to other people, they will have a more positive picture in their minds. So, the more positive the statement, the more assertively you are communicating. You must conjure up a definite picture of exactly *how* you want them to take care. A request such as 'Could you hold this with both hands and keep it level?' gives a specific picture of exactly what you want.

Working out what you want

You need, therefore, to communicate positively and specifically exactly what it is that you want. If you have trouble working this out for yourself positively and specifically, you could try the following three steps:

a) Pinpoint what you do *not* want.

b) Consider what your ideal preference is as an alternative to the 'don't want'. Try to be specific.

c) Consider what you would be prepared to settle for.

Setting the scene

First decide on the most relevant person to whom you should make your wants or needs known. This should be the person who can do something about it; there's no point in complaining to someone who is not directly involved. Make sure you have their full attention before you make your statement. You may need to arrange a time and place to talk to them. In an off-the-cuff situation, calling them by name and allowing a silence to give them a chance to switch their attention to you is important. Touching an arm or a shoulder might sometimes be appropriate. For instance, Mary is having lunch with her colleague. He begins to read his paper, absorbed in his task. Mary says to him, 'Bill,' and waits for him to look up, which he does. 'There's something I wanted to say.'

Saying what you want

Then it is up to you to make a statement which clearly and concisely expresses what you want, with the relevant strength of feeling indicated by your body language and tone of voice. Remember to be positive and specific, and ensure that you speak for yourself rather than generalizing. Some of the following phrases could preface your request:

'I'd like you to . . .'
'I'd prefer you to . . .'
'Could you please . . . ?'
'Would you . . . ?'

Possible responses

There are a number of possible responses to a request and some may be easier to deal with than others. These could include:

- agreement (it is surprising how often this happens when we do pluck up the courage to be assertive)
- direct refusal
- suggested compromise
- agreement, but postponed to another time
- blustering excuses, but no direct refusal
- request ignored or no response
- sarcastic put-down
- sulks
- churlish complaints
- argumentative bait: attempts to sidetrack you or manipulate you
- aggressive attack

If you are faced with a response that is not satisfactory, you will need to persist in your request if it is important enough.

Persistence

There are two techniques in assertiveness training which are useful in persisting with a request; they can also be applied to other aspects of assertiveness, such as putting forward an opinion, a criticism and so on. These techniques are 'sticking to it' and 'reflecting the response'. Remember once again that your tone of voice, attitude to the other person and your emotional control are also vital.

Sticking to it: This merely involves repeating what you have to say over and over again until it has been heard, understood and taken seriously.

Reflecting the response and sticking to it: This involves:

- paying attention to what the other person has said.
- responding briefly to any *relevant* questions, ignoring those which are irrelevant.
- summarizing the main point of what the other person has said *very briefly*.
- always ending up with your 'sticking to it' statement.

When using one or both of these persistence techniques, it is important to keep body language and tone of voice relaxed and calm, although firm. The temptation is to get increasingly strident, aggressive, churlish or sarcastic each time you repeat your request. It is better to stay in the same 'gear' each time you repeat yourself, otherwise you will come over as aggressive rather than assertive.

The assertive approach to making a request and persisting with it can be contrasted with the three other approaches: aggression, submission and manipulation.

Aggressive approach

This includes:

- making a demand without giving people the chance to switch their attention from whatever they are doing.
- giving orders when a request would be more appropriate.
- blaming or accusing people of not having fulfilled the request in the past.

Submissive approach

This includes:

- grumbling or complaining behind the scenes because you are not getting what you want.
- failing to consider your own wants and needs at all.
- making a request in an unconvincing way so that the other person does not realize how important the request is to you.
- holding back from stating what you want or need.
- giving up the request at the first hurdle.

Manipulative approach

This includes:

- using insincere ego-boosting to get what you want.
- dropping hints.
- making veiled threats.
- trying to make others feel guilty in order to get them to do what you want.
- speaking for others as opposed to just speaking for yourself.
- trying to convince others that they really want to do what you want.

I found these hints on becoming more assertive very useful indeed. It took me time to get into the rhythm of a more assertive approach in expressing my opinions. I found Meg's list of rights very useful and have constantly referred back to it. I began to notice that I became more objective, really listened, allowed time for the other point of view and found more frequently than in the past points on which I could agree with the other person. It began to feel as if other people were easier to have discussions with, but I have a feeling that it was a change in me.

5 Refusing, negotiating and cooperating

This section tells you how to respond assertively to requests made of you, and covers not only refusing outright but also negotiating and cooperating. Assertiveness is often wrongly assumed to be a matter of sticking to your guns, being stubbornly uncooperative. However, while there is a time and place for being assertively (even 'stubbornly') uncooperative, there is also a time for negotiating assertively. What is important is that you decide for yourself whether to say no, compromise or negotiate.

SAYING 'NO' ASSERTIVELY

Five steps to saying 'No'
You must remember that you have the right to say no – and so do others. There are five points to remember about saying no assertively.

(1) Take time to decide exactly what you *really do want* with regard to the request being made of you. You need to take into account your gut reaction to it; if you get that sinking feeling, it means that in your heart of hearts you really do not want to comply with the request. Take time to make up your mind.

(2) Make sure you have all the information you need before you make the decision. Ask for any information you do not have.

(3) If you decide to turn down the request, remember that you are only turning down the request, not rejecting the person.

(4) Make a short clear statement that shows you are firmly but gently turning down the request. Try to include the word 'no' whenever possible; if not, you must make absolutely sure that what you are saying is interpreted as a clear refusal, avoiding any prevarication and using assertive body language and tone of voice.

> 'No. I'm not prepared to . . .'
> 'I'd prefer not to . . .'
> 'No, I'm not willing to . . .'
> 'The answer is "No" . . .'

(5) Persist in the refusal by using the techniques for persistence outlined in the previous section: that is, 'sticking to it' and 'reflecting the response'.

Appropriate embellishments

Occasionally it is totally appropriate to give a brief 'No' answer without any additions: for instance, when people already know your reasons, or when they try to manipulate you or goad you into a wordy argument. A brief refusal and persistent repetition may be the most effective strategy. However, in many situations you may feel it is more appropriate, polite or humane to add some embellishment to the basic 'No'. In these cases, you should try to keep your additions short and to the point. You need to deal with your anxiety in saying no by taking your time and then keeping your reply short.

Giving a reason

Sometimes it is relevant to give a reason, and sometimes it is not. It may sound blunt or hurtful not to give one in some situations; in others, a reason is just unnecessary delay. Having explained your reason once, there is no need to repeat or justify it though expert manipulators or aggressive people will try to invalidate it. Often the other person may not be entitled to a reason, particularly for a personal decision.

Apologies

Sometimes it is appropriate and assertive to make an apology. It is generally recommended that apologies should be genuine in order to be assertive. However, many people are used to giving apologies which are not totally sincere in order to be polite. If you habitually use apologies in this way, you may find it easier to say no by putting in an occasional 'I'm sorry' in order to feel that you are being polite. But it is important to notice if you are beginning to overdo it and sliding towards being over-apologetic, which is submissive.

Suggesting alternatives

Sometimes it might be appropriate to suggest an alternative. You may prefer to agree to the request at another time or place and want to suggest alternatives to suit you. Or you may know that someone else might be genuinely interested in complying with the request. One pitfall here is in agreeing to arrange the alternative before you have established that it is possible. I once did this by enthusiastically agreeing to arrange speakers from the Trust in varying locations around the country. I ended up having to fulfil the obligations myself with the result that I was exhausted for the following week's activities.

Concern about others' feelings
It may be appropriate to explain to someone that you do not intend to hurt their feelings by saying no. This expression of concern needs to be genuine in order to be assertive and have the desired effect.

Coping with the guilt of saying no
There seem to be times when most people feel guilty at saying no. Often this guilt is based on one or both of the following beliefs:

- other people are too weak to cope with my refusal.
- other people's wants/needs/priorities must come before my own.

However, you must remember:
- other people may, or may not, be hurt by your refusal; either way, most people are strong enough to cope and to accept your 'No'.
- You are important too. You are responsible for deciding your own priorities.

It is useful to consider the negative consequences of *not* saying no. These can include:

- being exploited and treated as a pushover.
- not getting the respect you deserve from others.
- degrading people by assuming they cannot cope with your refusal.
- hating yourself for being weak.
- resenting people who make requests of you.
- spending your time on other people's priorities and responsibilities rather than your own.
- getting little satisfaction out of your job or your life because you spend your time doing other people's cast-off tasks.
- not having the chance to develop your own talents and abilities because you are too busy doing what other people want you to do.

- lowering the standard of your work because you become exhausted by trying to be superhuman and doing everything that people ask you to do.
- becoming depressed as the backlog of resentment gets turned in on yourself.
- becoming a victim or martyr and bringing out the worst in even the nicest people because you do not know your own limits.

Saying no can be stressful in the short term because it is difficult to do, but the long-term risks of not saying no are even greater.

Saying no aggressively

This approach includes:

- refusing for the sake of being difficult, or to get the better of someone, or to retaliate for their having said no to you in the past.
- using words and a tone of voice which demonstrate an inappropriately high strength of feeling, or which attack or put down the other person.
- displaying a lack of respect for the other person's right to ask for what she wants.

Saying no submissively

This approach includes:

- saying yes when you would really rather say no or when your own judgment tells you that it is better to say no.
- avoiding a decision and letting it slide until, in the end, you have to cooperate because there is no time to arrange for someone else to do it.
- perhaps initially managing to say no, but in an unconvincing or over-apologetic way, then allowing yourself to be talked into something.
- finding that, having agreed against your better judgment, you have no time to carry out the request and have to let the person down after all.
- carrying out a request faultily, late or with bad grace, full of grumbles or sulks; complaining behind the scenes about being put upon.

Saying no manipulatively

This approach includes:

- trying to make the other person feel guilty for asking.
- persuading the other person to seek an alternative, perhaps with charm, ego-boosting or flirting.
- avoiding a direct refusal, but sidetracking or blustering with lots of lengthy excuses in the hope that the other person will give up asking.
- not taking responsibility for the decision, but citing someone else's disapproval or quoting policies.
- making veiled threats or indirectly putting down the other person for asking.

ASSERTIVE NEGOTIATION

Saying no and persisting in saying no should be the uncooperative aspect of assertiveness. But that is not the end of it; assertiveness can also mean compromise and negotiation, or total cooperation if that is what you choose. So, assertiveness includes:

- assertive non-cooperation: sticking to your guns.
- assertive compromise: negotiation.
- assertive cooperation: saying yes.

Eight negotiating steps

Meg Bond showed me that assertive negotiation involves the following steps:

(1) Decide what your ideal preference is in the situation and decide how strongly you feel about that ideal preference.
(2) Decide what second preference you would be willing to settle for and how strongly you feel about it.
(3) Communicate your ideal preference and how strongly you feel about it to the other person.
(4) Find out what their ideal preference is and how strongly they feel about it.
(5) Take into account both your ideal preferences and how strongly both you and the other person feel about the situation, and then decide on whether it is appropriate to reveal your second preference.
(6) Try to find out what second preference the other person would be willing to settle for. Reveal what you would be willing to settle for and how strongly you feel about it.
(7) Establish a common agreement with the other person if possible.

(8) Stick to your guns about your second line of preference if the other person tries to push you beyond that.

ASSERTIVE COOPERATION

If you decide that you want to say yes and that you are able to follow through the agreement, it is assertive to cooperate.

When you agree to something, you need to ensure that you do indeed carry it out with good grace and without complaints. You have made a contract and assertiveness involves sticking to that contract unless you clearly indicate that you have changed your mind or realize that you have made a mistake in agreeing.

I found all this very useful and welcome advice. It helped in learning to say no to allow myself to take time. I followed the same course when negotiating and that was easier too – by the time I had talked myself through the steps I really knew when I could agree or be cooperative. It was truly worth the effort and time involved.

6 Giving and receiving feedback

So far we have mainly been learning ways of making requests and responding to them. This section continues with the two-way flow of assertive communication: giving and receiving feedback. We all need to have feedback from others around us. We need to know what effect we have on each other, otherwise assumptions are made and misunderstandings confuse communication, resulting in a build-up of stress.

The British are notoriously poor at giving feedback to each other; compliments and constructive criticism are rare, possibly because both can be difficult to give and respond to. We risk embarrassing or hurting ourselves or others. Yet the investment of short-term stress involved in giving feedback is worth the long-term stress reduction.

GIVING COMPLIMENTS

We expect high standards from people and often take their achievements for granted. More expressions of appreciation would probably change the atmosphere of the workplace. However, for a compliment to be assertive it must be made about something which we genuinely like or appreciate, and it must be given for its own sake rather than to achieve other ends.

ACCEPTING COMPLIMENTS

To be able to give good feedback, we have to learn what it feels like to be on the receiving end and how to accept a compliment without aggression, embarrassment or deference. Compliments are like gifts; if they are not accepted or are thrown back in the giver's face the giver may feel put down and be less likely to give again. Sometimes people think it is immodest to accept a compliment, so they try to give the credit to someone else or deny their own skill or expertise.

GIVING CRITICISM

Most of us find that both giving and receiving criticism is very stressful. When giving criticism, the chances are you are not going to be the recipient's favourite person, however constructively your criticism is given. Most people have experienced a lot of destructive criticism in the past and are likely to feel hurt, however tactful you are. Everyone needs to be liked, but as far as criticism is concerned, you need to ask yourself which is more important – being liked or getting the message across.

In the long term, someone who lets people know where she stands will be respected and probably liked more than someone with a non-assertive approach to criticism. You will also need to avoid 'the compassion trap'. If criticism is due, it is more humane in the long run to express it rather than let the person go on making the same mistake. You can be sensitive to other people's feelings up to a point, but you are not respecting them if you feel so sorry for them that you do not come out with constructive criticism at all.

Assertive approach
Assertive criticism includes the following features:

- making sure the criticism is given at the most appropriate time and place – that is, as soon as possible after the event and preferably face to face and in private. Try to make sure that there is time to give the other person a chance to respond rather than doing a brisk 'hit and run'.

- specifying exactly what the person has done (or not done) or exactly why the way they did it bothers you (it is important that you do not comment on their personality).

- saying how you feel about what they've done, indicating appropriate strength of feeling and speaking for yourself, using 'I' in phrases such as 'I'm worried', 'I feel cross', 'I'm concerned', or 'I feel furious'.

- stating exactly what you would prefer they do as an alternative.

- stating the positive consequences of their agreeing to your request (but being sure to carry through any promises).

- stating the negative consequences of their not agreeing to the request (but being sure to be prepared to carry through any specified action, so that you are not making an idle threat).

- stating how you feel about giving the criticism, such as embarrassment or awkwardness: for instance, 'I'm loath to stifle your enthusiasm, because you seem to be really enjoying working here.'

- persisting, if necessary, using 'sticking to it' and 'reflecting the response'. For example, 'I understand you're short of time but I'd prefer you . . .'

- ending on a positive note, perhaps expressing some appreciation of their listening or your relief at having got it out in the open or over with: 'I'm relieved you saw my point of view.'

If you used all these steps at once your criticism would be very wordy. The most important steps are:

- speaking in private, face to face
- commenting on behaviour, not personality
- stating what you want as an alternative

Other steps could be added as necessary and used to help you to persist when the criticism is important to you.

DEALING WITH CRITICISM

If you feel pretty terrible when you are criticized, you need not worry; you are not alone. Most people have been on the receiving end of plenty of criticism which has been badly given, unjust, badly timed, or just plain humiliating. So you might take it kindly if it is suggested that criticism can be useful. Even the most constructive, well-timed, supportive criticism can make you feel bad if you have been humiliated in the past. It is easy to over-react to someone who is being nasty. This section offers a few ways of dealing with criticism which might help you to get the most out of a situation in which you are being criticized.

Assertive approach

The first step is to decide whether there is any truth at all in the criticism. Categorize the criticism as 'I totally agree', 'I totally disagree', or 'I agree with part of it, but disagree with the rest'. However well or badly the criticism is phrased, the content is what you are paying attention to.

An assertive response includes being willing to accept valid criticism without defensive justifications, excuses, passing the buck and so on. A plain, direct, honest answer deals positively with the criticism and helps you let it sink in. If you start trying to talk or sidle your way out of it, you are likely to learn less. On the other hand, you can reject criticism with which you disagree without putting the other person down. Just because you feel they are putting you down is no reason to retaliate in like manner; instead, you should firmly contradict the critical statement. Thirdly, you may partially agree with the criticism; that is, there is some truth in it but it is overdone in some way. In this case, you will need to indicate the extent to which you disagree. Next, if there is any part of the criticism which you accept, tell the person exactly what it is you are agreeing with.

- *For example:* I agree, I don't speak up much. I could take part in the policy-making much more.'

Criticisms with which you disagree require a *positive* statement about yourself to contradict the inappropriately negative remark.

- *For example:* 'I disagree. I think I'm quite punctual.'

Lastly, for those criticisms with which you only partially agree, remember to confirm exactly what you agree with and specify exactly what you disagree with.

- *For example:* 'I partially agree. I do have my occasional fast and slow days, but on the whole I work at a steady pace. I'd call myself fairly consistent.'

Negative enquiry

Quite often people make generalizations when giving criticism; they say 'you always' do such and such, or label your personality.

'Negative enquiry' can help you find out exactly what actions or what approach has bothered someone, as well as helping you to discover the emotional effects of your actions. This knowledge can be taken into account the next time you act, or alternatively it can open up a useful discussion about viewpoints and values.

'Negative enquiry' means asking questions to elicit more useful details from the person who is criticizing you or who you think might be feeling critical of you without expressing it. The word 'negative' may look confusing here; however, this is the term you will find used in assertiveness textbooks. It indicates that you are asking the other person to tell you something critical. The enquiry is actually positive in the sense that you are enabling your critic to give *constructive* rather than destructive criticism. Constructive criticism is always helpful.

For instance, Linda, a student social worker, is told by the tutor that she has an 'unprofessional manner' with the clients. As it stands, this is not a particularly helpful comment since it is too general.

LINDA: I'm not clear what you mean . . . Can you give me an example?

TUTOR: Well, your relationships with the clients are often unprofessional.

LINDA: What exactly have I done or said which was unprofessional?

TUTOR: It's the way you talk to them – you're much too familiar.

LINDA: Could you give me more details? In what way familiar, exactly?

TUTOR: You call them all by their first names. Most of these clients are of a different generation: they don't like being addressed by their first names.

LINDA: I see. When I first came to this team one or two told me to call them by their first names, so I sort of assumed it was the done thing. I can see now I should check with each client and find out what she wants me to call her. Yes, I agree I wasn't very professional. I should be treating each person as an individual rather than making blanket assumptions. Is there anything else you thought I was being unprofessional about?

TUTOR: Well, no. That's about it, I think.

So, in that situation, what started out as an unhelpful bit of criticism eventually helped Linda to rethink her use of names. Linda's negative enquiry, rather than the original general statement, drew out exactly what the tutor meant.

7 Applying assertiveness

Having worked my way studiously through Meg Bond's assertiveness training, I had to admit to myself that it was fascinating, useful and very hard work. I had somehow thought in my innocence that everything would automatically fall into place just because I had read the words and agreed with most of them. This just did not happen – I had actually to do it. I had to practise.

As with tension control, I had to work at assertiveness most of the time and could not just put it to one side to bring out when needed. I had to put it into practice in public, so to speak, and once started I could not just stop and say, 'Sorry, I think I'll just try another approach', or 'Wait a moment I'll just say no in another way', or 'Can I take back that criticism, I cannot take the hassle'. I had to grit my teeth, put up with any embarrassment I felt and try again. Gradually it has become easier and now I believe I am almost beginning to fall into an assertive approach automatically.

It did, however, help to know that others had felt like me. As Meg Bond shows in the following list, when you learn more about the skills of assertiveness, you too may go through some of the following phases, although not necessarily in the same order.

- suspicion about assertiveness as a concept
- more understanding, particularly about the differences between assertiveness and aggressiveness
- relief at realizing that being assertive doesn't really mean becoming a nasty person
- realizing that you are already assertive a lot of the time
- a tendency to think that you don't need to practise assertiveness – that you are assertive all the time
- realizing that there are times – particularly when you're under stress – when you could, after all, learn to be more assertive
- becoming more aware of your own approach: for instance, body language, tone of voice, the things you say
- self-consciousness and embarrassment when you are aware of your own approach
- feeling stilted and false when you are trying out new assertive methods
- surprise when assertive methods are easier to use than you thought
- feeling bad when you make a mistake and feeling stupid; criticizing yourself too much

- feeling easier about being aware of your own approach; more self-acceptance
- feeling pleased with yourself when trying out assertiveness; noticing little successes
- feeling delight when realizing you've been assertive without consciously trying to be so, even in a difficult situation

PITFALLS

When learning and developing communication skills you will make mistakes; this is inevitable. However, there are three things to bear in mind:

- don't put yourself down because you have made a mistake.
- ask yourself what you have learned from making the mistake.
- apologize to anyone who was adversely affected by your mistake. You only need to apologize once. Do not slide into overdoing it, putting yourself down or grovelling.

Making mistakes is a natural part of the learning process. What is important is that you have enough self-confidence to allow yourself to learn from them. This may be easier said than done. One way of regaining lost self-confidence is to remind yourself of your successes, however small they may be.

SUCCESS IN ASSERTIVENESS

How do you measure the extent of your success in being assertive? Do you feel you have failed if you have not got exactly what you want? Consider that getting what you want is not the only measure of success in developing your assertive skills. Success can also be measured by other factors.

Self-respect

If you have been able to be a little more assertive in a situation where you might previously have been submissive, aggressive or manipulative, then you are likely to feel a sense of achievement at having made some progress. Your sense of self-respect will be enhanced by reminding yourself of this achievement.

Communicating clearly

Getting your point across is a success. If you have clearly communicated that you feel strongly about something but you still don't get what you want, at least people will realize that they have gone against your wishes on this occasion. Next time they may be more likely to take you into account. You will be noticed as a person who has a point of view and who can express it. Most people can easily get wrapped up in and preoccupied with their own thoughts, priorities, feelings and goals; being assertive means that you are more likely to be seen, heard, understood and taken into account by those around you.

Getting what you want
This may happen more often than you might expect if you are used to being non-assertive. On many occasions your assertiveness will be part of the natural flow of clear communication. Other people will know what your point of view is and what you want, and can more easily take that into account without any fuss. At other times there may be a fuss, but if something is important enough to you, it will be worth it.

CHAPTER 4

Avoidance

Consultants:

CRIME PREVENTION UNIT
Metropolitan Police

LYNNE HOWELLS
Training Consultant,
Women's Unit, Birmingham City Council

Aggression takes physical as well as verbal forms. There are some positive straightforward steps you can take to help you avoid confrontation. You are in danger of allowing yourself to be an easy target if you do not bother to take simple precautions. Remember that an assailant relies on opportunity, stealth and surprise. Most people out to attack someone are nervous; they do not want to get caught, marked or hurt themselves. So you can take steps to avoid being the obvious 'pushover' they are likely to choose. This of course applies to everyone and indeed statistics prove that most attacks are by young men on young men; but for the purposes of this book I am thinking mainly of women. We can all benefit from the following advice, and that includes myself.

1 Self-protection

To help me learn the safety measures of which I have been so ignorant until now, I sought the help of the Metropolitan Police and Lynne Howells who works on 'Strategies for Strength' for Birmingham City Council. There is of course no copyright on common sense, but somehow it is one sense which, as far as I am concerned, seems to bury its head in the sand. Following these guidelines, I learned a great deal.

As Kalegh Quinn says in *Stand Your Ground* (1983), her excellent book for Channel Four:

> 'Self-preservation is a continuing process of awareness. Once this process has started, it spreads into all aspects of your life, leads you to re-evaluate everything, increases your understanding of what is happening to you, your control over your life and your willpower.'

It was not until my daughter Suzy was abducted on that bright July day that it occurred to me that she or anyone could be in danger in the middle of the day while doing a routine job. Indeed, it was not until I was sitting in front of a television camera doing a live broadcast about women in the workplace that I fully realized the risk that she had been taking and the now inconceivable way that she and I had nonchalantly neglected to face some glaring facts. It was at that moment that I vowed to enable every working woman to have the opportunity to help herself.

First of all we need to look at ourselves: I will give you four 'A's which may help you to remember them.

AWARENESS

Since starting the Trust I have been invited to talk to many different organizations from the BMA to associations of veterinary surgeons, farmers' wives and temporary secretaries. I have never ceased to be amazed by the stories I have heard (often told for the first time) which are nearly always followed by the statement, 'I never thought it could happen to me – I thought I was streetwise', or 'I always thought it was the sort of thing which happened to other people'.

Unfortunately, galling though it is for us to accept limitations, we have to face the fact that none of us is invincible. It would be good to feel that we could go about our business when and how we choose, free from fear of abuse. Of course we need to be able to work to the best of our abilities in whatever job we wish, even if this means travelling on our own and being out at night, but we would be foolish to ignore the possible dangers this entails.

Awareness is the key. Women should not be frightened into taking ridiculous steps in the name of self-protection. A few precautions such as letting people know where you are when you are out of the office, avoiding potentially risky situations, carrying a personal alarm in your hand when you go home at night – these will help you feel safer, and that is important because confidence is vital.

Consciously build up in yourself confidence in your own strength and power. You are likely to be much stronger and faster than you realize. Most people never test themselves to find out what they can really do. Part of self-preservation is having a good idea of your physical capabilities. Being fit is an important help. As co-founder of the British Slimnastics Association, where I have seen so many women blossom and thrive with our Whole Person Approach to Fitness, I have no doubt that it pays to exercise and eat healthily. You will benefit from classes whatever your age or abilities, not only in fitness but also in building up your morale, which is more than worth the effort.

It helps to listen to success stories. Talk to your friends, discuss this with your colleagues, read the papers. There are many stories of women who have survived attacks. There are also many instances when people have dealt with threatening situations extremely well, but because they felt frightened and out of control they were unable to recognize the skills they used.

Lynne Howells told me how staff from Birmingham City Council began to talk about such situations, look at what had happened and identify the skills they had used. They found the relief of talking together enormous and this in itself proved a tremendous confidence-booster. She considers this particularly important in work situations because often the dominant feeling is that to talk about attacks is a sign of professional failure. Silence contributes to keeping a lid on the overall problem at the same time as it does precisely the opposite of what was intended – it raises the level of fear. In Lynne's experience, ignorance of the facts feeds fertile imaginations.

One of Lynne's course members told this story: 'I was working in the kitchen [of a residential establishment] when one of the residents came in brandishing a knife. I carried on talking and working and calmly asked him to hand me the knife to chop up the vegetables.' This woman was shocked, but calmly and sensibly she defused the aggression and removed the danger. Unthinkingly, she used many skills. You, too, are probably better equipped than you know.

ALERTNESS

Stand up tall, keep your feet slightly apart for good balance, keep your head up and your mind focused on your surroundings. If you look like someone who knows what is going on around you, you look less vulnerable. Try to look confident without appearing arrogant.

It is interesting to note the research done in the 1970s by a famous psychologist, Betty Grayson. Using a hidden camera, Betty Grayson filmed random pedestrians walking down a street. She then showed the film to some convicted muggers who were in prison, and asked them to rate the pedestrians for 'assaultability'. The convicts did not necessarily pick women over men, girls over boys, or old people over young people. They went for people who looked vulnerable because of the way they walked. The typical 'muggable' person swung their arms out of rhythm with their legs, they plonked their feet down on the pavement with a graceless thump instead of the swinging walk which most people have, and they generally looked physically unbalanced. Other observers of 'muggable' types have noticed that they tend to be in a daze or a daydream, to walk hunched over, and to pay no attention to their surroundings, often looking lost. This description does not refer to people who are disabled. On the contrary, people with disabilities are often very much 'in touch' with their own bodies and extremely good at knowing their physical strengths and weaknesses. This is something we would all do well to emulate. A 1979 census survey found that most mugging victims were young men, the group you might expect to be safest.

Exercise classes will help your posture and the relaxation techniques outlined in Chapter 1 will help you breathe easily and avoid being handicapped by tension.

ASSESS AND ACT

These last two 'A's are your vital triggers. You already possess the physical abilities to put them into operation.

One of my jobs is to teach swimming to adults who have suffered some trauma like nearly drowning, or maybe have developed a fear of water early in childhood, or escaped their swimming lessons because of illness. Others come because they have some disability and swimming is recommended. For most of my students, learning to swim for the first time, or being able to move without pain or difficulty, is a joy, and this feeling tends to soften their natural caution. I take great care to teach them that total confidence in the water is folly. Water is a foreign element which we must respect. Every time we go swimming or accompany others who are swimming, it is sensible to assess the situation, assess the safety and any means of rescue and then reassess what we feel we could or should do in an emergency. I teach my students to do this consciously until it becomes an automatic reaction.

I believe you should do this in the workplace too. Travelling to, from and for work, choosing what work to do and who to work for, working with your colleagues and for your boss, going out of the office, working in your home and going into other people's, all should be consciously assessed, reassessed and then reassessed again. You should know what is expected of you by your employer, and how you yourself are able and prepared to behave. And if you feel uncomfortable around a person or a place, if a warning signal goes off somewhere deep inside you, if you feel scared or even just uneasy, do not ignore it. Act upon it straight away.

Instinct, intuition – call it what you will – is very valuable. We need to redefine these gifts and recognize them for the source of strength and power which they are. Many women ignore their instinct . . .

There are many times when women have said, after being in a threatening situation, 'I knew there was something wrong, but I thought I was imagining it', or 'I told myself not to be silly'.

Intuition is easy to ignore. It's hard to define; society places greater confidence on reason and logic. Intuition becomes something almost mystical and attributed to the female, and therefore not to be trusted. If we have been taught not to put ourselves first, to meet other people's needs before our own, to be 'nice', we may learn to mistrust our own gut responses and give other people the benefit of the doubt. This is particularly true in work where policies and procedures take precedence over instinctive feelings of right and wrong, and so it can be harder to put into practice. This is compounded by the fact that the philosophy of 'the customer is always right' makes it difficult for staff to say when a customer is crossing the boundary of acceptable behaviour.

Managers may fear that greater awareness and confidence in staff will widen the gap between them and the customer. However, the experience of council workers in Birmingham shows that greater staff awareness and confidence means that customers receive a better service. By listening to our instincts we are better able to assess situations and, more important, to assess the appropriate response.

This intuitive sense is the key to avoiding potentially aggressive situations. We need to be in touch with our senses and our own particular responses, and have the confidence to trust them. Usually the body is the first to respond when something is wrong; stomach churning, dry throat, tenseness in back and shoulders. Nothing may be obvious to the reason, yet the feeling that something is wrong is very powerful.

> 'I went to see this client at home. He didn't say or do anything threatening but I could feel prickles up my back. When I got back to the office, I told my manager that this man should be seen by two social workers in the office, not at home. Luckily my manager respected my judgment. Since then this man has been accused of murdering a young girl.'
>
> Social worker, Birmingham

This kind of openness at work is not usual, and yet as the illustration shows it can be a useful starting point in assessing a situation and helping us feel more secure. When we are in tune with our feelings and reactions we are equipped to act promptly. With practice our actions will be instinctive or automatic.

So now you need to learn the actions. There are many guidelines: you may already follow many of them and some you will forget, but take them slowly – assess, reassess and act.

2 Reducing the risks

The ideas below are sensible, straightforward precautions and easy to put into practice. You may feel that they interfere with your personal liberty. That of course is a matter of choice for you. However, I think you will find that they will not interfere with your job, and will in fact help you to feel safer and more in control. This in turn will enable you to concentrate more on your work, and that is the aim of this book.

Do remember that although I have been helped by many experts in the compilation of these lists, they are in no way foolproof. (It would be very difficult indeed to avoid a determined attacker.) But they will reduce the risks. You may find them incomplete and be able to add ideas of your own. If you do, please let us all know – the more we can be open and share our thoughts and come to each other's aid the more likely we are to reduce the opportunities for attack or abuse.

TRAVELLING TO, FROM, OR FOR WORK

First of all: *make sure you do not present yourself as an Easy Target.*

- Know where you are going and look as if you want to get there. If necessary, look up your route beforehand, assess any difficulties such as desolate areas, docklands, etc., and make any necessary changes. Make a note of the roads, and keep that and the address plus the telephone number easily to hand.

- Wear shoes that are easy to walk in and ensure that you can run if necessary. They should be secure and give you good balance. I remember seeing a girl run over just because she wore high-heeled boots; she took a risk and then simply could not move fast enough. If you are wearing 'fashion' shoes you should be prepared to kick them off and abandon them in order to defend yourself or run away. You may feel it is necessary to move silently, so choose your footwear accordingly. One secretary told me that she always had to walk down an alleyway to reach her house after coming back from a disco. It was a well-known haunt for boys looking for 'fair game'. She was convinced that they waited until they heard the tap-tap-tap of high heels. She would take off her shoes before she came into earshot, and then creep through the alley to her home; she was never mugged or molested.

- Avoid clothes that can hinder your movements: tight skirts that will stop you running or kicking; bits and pieces that can be used to restrain or strangle you; wide-brimmed hats, hood, sunglasses, open umbrellas which can all obscure your vision and make you more vulnerable. It also makes sense to wear clothes that reflect the fact that going to work is uppermost in your mind. Although we all have the right to wear anything we like at any time there are a number of unwritten rules about clothes and unconsciously we may send out messages which invite trouble. For instance, wearing a coat to cover up revealing or skimpy clothes or an emotive uniform, such as that of a nurse, makes sense, especially at night; so does not having jewellery outwardly on show.

- Try to keep both hands free. Never carry heavy bags in both hands at the same time. Whenever possible carry nothing. Do not walk with both hands thrust into your pockets.

- If you have to carry things, try to use a bag that will go over your shoulder. Use a small one slung across your body under a jacket or coat, or a shoulder bag with a short strong strap and good fastenings. Make sure it sits close to your body with the fastenings innermost.

- If you must carry a handbag or clutchbag, do not hold it too tightly to your body. This could indicate that it contains something of value.

- Be prepared to give your bag up. This means that you should be careful not to carry your whole important world wherever you go. I often think that Filofaxes and their ilk have a lot to answer for. They can become so precious that their owners cling to the bag containing these reams of information at the expense of their own safety. All irreplaceable documents should be duplicated if at all possible. Leave behind anything you do not really need. Practise in your mind allowing your bag to go free – for most of us it is a reflex action to hold on like grim death. One of my more elderly students had her bag snatched by a youth in a car. She hung on and was dragged twenty yards before she let go, getting a broken thigh and a scarred face all for the sake of a bag.

- Place essential valuables such as wallets in an inside pocket secured with a safety pin. This is an infallible way to stop a pickpocket.

- Do not wear a scarf with ends hanging down the back. These could be used to strangle you. If possible, tuck the scarf out of sight.

- Carry your own 'weapons' – keep an awareness alarm at the ready in your hand or pocket and be prepared to use it. The best ones can be thrown to one side after they are activated. It will be hard for the attacker to choose whether to stop the noise, continue to pursue you or make a rapid exit. Develop your own noise too. A loud deep shout is very effective: you rarely have to fiddle for it, drop it or even lose it, so it is crucial to practise it. Combs, shoes and umbrellas can all be effective. The law demands that any item must not be carried for the sole purpose of self-defence, but a handful of small coins or a bunch of keys can be fairly formidable.

- If you suspect that you have had too much to drink to get home safely, put aside your pride and ask a friend of long standing to accompany you, or take a taxi. If necessary, phone a relative, flatmate or friend and ask them to pick you up. Be prepared to reciprocate the gesture – we all need help sometimes!

- Use caution in conversation with, or being overheard by, male strangers. Avoid giving your name, address or place of employment, or revealing you live alone. When Suzy was just eleven years old she went with her friend Evelyn for her first visit to town without an accompanying adult. They were going to the V & A and I thought I had given them every precaution under the sun. They carried them through with care, but on the bus coming home Suzy mentioned to her friend that as she was tired she would go back home even though her mother was still teaching. She was followed back by the couple who were sitting behind the two girls. Luckily, I had in fact arrived home already and when they rang the doorbell and asked the unsuspecting girl if they could use the toilet I put my head out of the window and they fled. I am ashamed to say that it took me some time to realize the importance of the incident and by the time I came to ringing the police I had no idea what the couple looked like.

- Remember that the slightest amount of alcohol can affect your judgment of both people and situations. Know your own limits.

- For the sake of your ease of mind and those you care about, leave behind in an obvious place all the details you think would be needed by the police if anything unfortunate did happen. When Suzy disappeared, we found that the lack of this information caused us some of the greatest hassle and distress. She was so fit she rarely went to the doctor and had not visited a hospital for years. She knew her blood group, but we had never known it; it was not available even through her dentist and she took that vital piece of information with her. She had just had her hair redone and we had no up-to-date portrait pictures of her. We could not in the trauma accurately remember all her characteristics, all of which are quite essential to the police. My husband Paul and I ended up by having to have our blood taken at the police station in front of witnesses. It then had to go away to a laboratory to be processed so that a particularly gruesome torso which had been found could be proved *not* to be Suzy. We knew the results could only prove a negative and not a positive, and they took a long time to come through. All this would have been much easier if we had had some record on which we could call. Do remember that although it might be very useful, in the event of an accident, to have these vital statistics on your person (in, say, your Filofax), it is no use at all if that too is destroyed or disappears with you. Leave all this information behind *as well*, and in an accessible identifiable place.

On foot

- If it is dark, in the early morning as well as at night, walk purposefully at a good pace and keep to well-lit busy streets.

- At all times of day avoid deserted places, dark buildings, bushes, waste ground, car parks and alleyways especially when you are walking on your own.

- Vary your daily travel routine – avoid a very regular pattern of movements.

- Familiarize yourself with your routes and surroundings. This will make it easier for you to avoid danger spots and to know where you might be able to seek help if you ever need it. Get to know where there are concealed entrances, and where the lighting is bad, where there are pubs or garages or public phones which might be useful should you think you are being followed.

- Be prepared to walk a long way round if necessary. It is a temptation to let laziness or haste cloud your judgment. It is not worth taking the risk.

- Try not to pass through a subway on your own; take advantage of other people who are passing the same way to act as your escort.

- If the street is deserted, walk down the middle of the pavement, face the oncoming traffic to avoid kerb crawlers and remain alert to your immediate surroundings. If you need to pass through a 'risk area' occupy your thoughts by actively thinking about what you would do if faced by a problem. Look for escape routes and be prepared to take action if necessary. If the pavement is narrow walk on the kerbside to avoid being grabbed by someone in a doorway.

- Carry your keys in your pocket ready to open up the office or your front door, and let yourself in quickly. Never put your name and address on the ring. Avoid keeping the keys in your bag; losing them if you are mugged adds insult to injury. If they are stolen with your bag, which will usually contain your name and address, change your locks *immediately*.

- At night, unless it is absolutely essential, do not use a pocket torch – this will show up your presence and make it more difficult for you to see a potential assailant. It is better to let your eyes become accustomed to the dark. It is useful, however, to carry a torch so that you can check your car before getting into it.

- Keep your awareness alarm in your hand when you walk home at night. Be prepared to use it.

- Keep enough money on you for a cab home if necessary. Use black taxis or other licensed cabs, or a minicab firm known locally for its good reputation.

- If you work in a secluded or undesirable area, organize a lift-share system with friends or colleagues. Ensure they wait until you have safely entered your home.

- It is folly to hitch-hike however desperate you are. I cringe now when I remember how I used to thumb for lifts and the risks I took. Again, it is not worth it. All of us are open to attack – play safe.

- Never be tempted to accept a lift with a stranger even if you are wet, tired or very late. This applies even if the driver claims to be a taxi or minicab – anyone who reads the news will remember that this can have disastrous consequences.

- If you do think that you are being followed, trust your instincts and take action. As confidently as you can, cross over the road, turning as you do so, in order to see whoever is behind you. If he crosses too, be prepared to recross again and again. Keep moving. If he continues to follow you make for a busy area – a pub, service station or other public premises, go in and phone the police and a friend. Also tell the publican, cashier or anyone else who is likely to help you.

- Beware of a stranger who warns you of the dangers of walking alone and then offers to accompany you. This is a ploy some attackers have been known to use.

- Attackers do not like noise, and when their stealth is compromised by a shrill alarm or a yell from you they may well beat a hasty retreat. If this fails, do not rely on other people coming to your aid because of the din. If you make it quite plain that you do not know the man or men concerned you may get assistance. Aim to break away as soon as possible and run into a group containing women – you are more likely to get help and less likely to run into a second problem.

- Be prepared to bang on doors and keep yelling even if you only suspect you are in danger. The verbal abuse you may arouse will certainly be better than a sexual attack.

- If you get no response, shout an instruction such as 'Phone the police' – people are likely to react when given something to do. In extreme situations, a heavy object such as a stone thrown through a window will invariably bring instant investigation.

- If you jog to work you may have some advantages. You will be wearing the ideal clothing to get away from someone quickly and you may be fitter than your pursuer – but do not bank on it. Wearing personal stereo headphones prevents you from hearing a would-be attacker (or traffic for that matter). Leave them at home.

- If you bicycle to work you have the advantage of being able to move fairly swiftly but otherwise you are no safer than on foot. All the above points apply to cyclists too.

Public transport
- Make sure you have the right change on you for the bus/train/tube/ phone. It is a good idea to have a phone card on you too.

- Waiting for a bus/tube/train at night, always try to stand in a well-lit place near groups of people, preferably including women. Walk on from isolated bus stops if necessary.

- When you get on to the vehicle try to sit near the guard, the conductor or other women passengers.

- If you find yourself alone on public transport with someone who you sense might harass you, why not try making yourself look as repulsive as possible. My co-founder of the BSA, Pamela Nottidge, recommends picking your nose. You could also try cleaning out your ears, scratching or muttering to yourself; your inhibitions are less important than your safety!

- If you find yourself molested in a train/tube/bus or in a public place do not hesitate to make a fuss straight away. One of my students grabbed the hand which seemed to be fondling her when she was packed like a sardine in a tube during rush hour. She quickly pulled it up above her head and said loudly to her startled swaying fellow travellers 'Who belongs to this?' She was surprised at how many men left the carriage at the next stop. It is vital to act quickly and not wait until the man has you alone.

- If you are attacked on a tube, try to wait until you reach the next station before pulling the communication cord as you will receive help more quickly. Run through the interconnecting doors if necessary. On a train do not be afraid to pull the emergency cord *immediately* to alert the driver or guard.

- When getting off trains attach yourself to people leaving the station. Deserted stations provide opportunities for thieves and other criminals. If no one is there, walk briskly. The same applies to tubes and buses.

By car
- Park your car in a place from which you know it will be safe to retrieve it for the journey home. Make sure the area is a well-lit public place, or a car park that is well attended and frequently in use. Lock up the car carefully, making sure that any valuables are out of sight in the boot.

- When you return to the car, have your car keys ready in your hand. Before you get in check that there is no one hiding in the back.

- When driving on your own, lock all the doors. Some people feel safer if they have the driver's door unlocked so that they can get out quickly in case of an accident. Choose the way which seems safest to you.

- If you are sitting in a car, lock all the doors and keep the windows shut or at least almost shut; use quarter lights for ventilation.

- Do not give lifts to hitch-hikers. It's sad to say it but even women on their own can be decoys.

- Do not stop to help a stranded motorist. Drive to the next telephone and call for assistance.

- The same applies if you see an accident on the road. Do not stop unless you are quite sure you are qualified. You are likely to be much more help if you get the services there quickly.

- If you think you are being followed try alerting other drivers by flashing your lights and sounding your horn. In any event drive on until you reach a police station, garage or other busy place.

- Know where you are going and keep a map handy, with a pocket torch to help you, so that you do not need to stop and ask for directions.

- Keep your car in good working order, carry extra petrol in a special safety-approved portable petrol tank, keep some change for a payphone in the glove compartment. I am ashamed to say that I once ran out of petrol on the M25 when I was going to give a talk. It was the most terrifying experience and one that I would hate to go through again.

- A car phone might be invaluable to a busy executive who has to travel a long way from base in unfamiliar surroundings. When using these, however, remember that it is easy to intercept the wavelengths and be careful when giving out private messages.

- Learn how to change a wheel so that you do not have to approach strangers to help you. We could all benefit from having basic knowledge of the inside of our cars.

- Save up and join the AA or RAC so that if you do break down you can phone for reliable and fairly prompt assistance.

By minicab

- Before you leave your home or place of work to go out for the evening, make sure you have with you the telephone number of a reputable minicab company. Just in case you miss the last bus or a promised lift, you know that you will still get home safely.

- When you book your minicab, ask the company for the name of the driver they are sending. When he arrives to collect you, ask him to tell you his name and the name of his minicab company to check that he really is the man sent for the job.

- Get in the back of the minicab.

- Try to share the cab with a friend – it's cheaper and safer.

- Although it's natural to chat with your driver, don't give away any information about your personal habits – where you work, who you live with, etc.

- If your driver is taking an unusual route to your destination or even travelling in the wrong direction, tactfully ask him to take a short cut to get you where you want to go.

- If you feel uncomfortable with your driver, ask him to drop you off in a well-lit, busy place with which you are familiar, where you can go for safety. Claim to feel car sick if it makes it any easier.

- If your destination is your home, ask the driver to drop you a couple of doors away – he doesn't need to know your exact address.

- When you arrive at your destination, have cash ready to pay the driver. Get out of the car as soon as you arrive, and then pay the driver through his window.

- Have your front-door keys ready in your pocket, and enter your home as quickly as possible.

- Before you use any minicab company, check that they are a respectable firm which you are happy to use. Ask your friends if they know of them, check that they're listed in the telephone directory or even go to see what their offices look like.

- Think ahead about how you would protect yourself in the exceptional instance of harassment, robbery or assault.

- If anything happens which makes you feel uncomfortable, get the driver's name and registration number and report it to his company. Should the worst happen, go to the police.

- Remember, most minicab drivers are reliable and honest. The last thing on their mind is trying to harm you. They simply want to provide you with a good service and a safe journey to your destination.

Coming home
- Put your porch light on to a time switch so that it gives you a good light should you return home after dark.

- When you get near your home, look up and down the street, stairs or corridor before standing still to unlock your door. Do not fiddle around at the door – concentrate on unlocking. Stay alert and get inside as quickly as possible.

- If you return home to find your doors or windows tampered with, leave immediately. Call the police from a neighbour's house or the nearest callbox. Do not attempt to tackle the intruder.

FINDING A JOB
- Remember that some careers carry with them special risks, often for both men and women. Social workers, doctors, estate agents, police officers, journalists, housing officers, all make visits to the houses of strangers, often at times of tension or high expectation. It is important to realize that the very reasons people like their work can be the same ones that create risks – autonomy, flexibility, helping people. You need to assess for yourself whether you are equipped, able and prepared to cope with these situations as well as with the work.

- There are some obvious pitfalls which can be avoided, such as advertisements offering an astonishing amount of money for very little work (such as modelling). Avoid escort agencies. They may be reputable in themselves but cannot really vet their clients.

- There are few dangers in applying to large companies with personnel departments but jobs advertised in newsagents or in the paper need careful checking, especially if they do not give an address or a company name.

- If you seek work through an agency it is probably wise to follow Brook Street's Ten Point Plan:
    1 Establish the credentials of the recruiting company.
    2 Always go to a reputable agency which establishes that clients are bona fide, has visited the premises and will provide a detailed job description.
    3 Always ensure the interview takes place at an office, of either the employer or the agency.
    4 If, for special reasons, this is not possible, ensure that the interview is in a public place, e.g. a hotel coffee lounge. Confirm those circumstances with the agency and make sure a companion can be on hand, at a safe distance.
    5 If in doubt, refuse to go to the interview.
    6 If it is necessary to attend an interview outside working hours, organize a friend to collect you at a specified time, and ensure that the interviewer is aware that someone is coming.
    7 Always make sure that someone knows where you are being interviewed.
    8 During an interview, steer the conversation away from personal subjects that bear no relevance to the job.
    9 No matter how well the interview appears to be going, avoid continuing discussions over dinner, drinks, etc.
    10 Ensure you have some form of transport – train, bus, car, taxi – to take you home. Never accept a lift from the interviewer.

- If you are tempted to take a job abroad, check out your employer and the work you will be expected to do before you go. Make sure that you will be suitably and safely accommodated when you get there. Inform everyone you can with all the details of addresses, names, etc., before you leave.

- Ask prospective employers whether they have procedures for protecting the safety of their employees. Most reputable firms consider this a vital part of staff relations.

- Understand for yourself quite clearly why you are being employed. Have you got the job because of your qualifications, your expertise, your potential or your personality or looks? Each reason may be perfectly valid, but it is important for you to be aware so that you can decide whether you are equipped, able and prepared to cope with the risks attached.

At work

- Always keep someone informed of your whereabouts. Tell a colleague if you are going to be out, write in your desk diary where you are and whom you are with, leaving a contact number if possible. If you are going on from one meeting to another, especially if the second is unscheduled, ring in to the office and let someone know. *Do not take your diary with you* or if you do make sure it is a duplicate. I am horrified by the number of media people who carry everything about themselves: their working time, their interview arrangements, telephone numbers, all holed up in the one briefcase. I cannot bear to think of the trauma if the briefcase were lost. And it would be extremely difficult to trace a missing person if all this information went too.

- If a stranger rings to arrange a meeting, it should be a routine procedure to call him back to check the validity of the company, his address, telephone number, etc.

- If a meeting in a secluded place cannot be avoided, have an exit route planned and work out in advance a means of transport back. Make sure you sit near the door; if there is no seat move one there. If possible avoid going into the centre of the building. If in any doubt about the situation make an excuse and leave.

- On arrival at any meeting about which you feel dubious, ask to ring your office and leave a contact number. Make it obvious that others know where you are. Arrange a 'distress' coding so that when you report by telephone you can alert help without compromising your safety.

- Avoid after-hours meetings.

- Do not give your home phone number or address to clients.

- If harassed by a colleague or a client, tell your superiors and make sure your complaint is taken seriously.

- Travelling, especially to trade shows, sales meetings and conferences, can pose problems for women because on these occasions many male colleagues do not simply put control on one side, they just decide not to be in control. On these occasions it is wise to keep control of yourself. Wear clothes (including those for evening parties) which give out the signals you intend to give out. Beware of flirting or getting into compromising situations, and do not drink more than you would at a business lunch.

- Lastly, and this is a cry from a mother's heart, while loyalty in your work is an essential part of professionalism, do not be over-secretive about problems with your clients or colleagues, or information about which you are worried. Hints are not good enough if you should suddenly disappear. Leave behind you a diary or a best friend who can keep your thoughts confidential except in an emergency.

In lifts

- When in doubt, use the stairs. Attackers can trap people in the lifts of apartment buildings, public buildings and offices. They can either stop the elevator between floors in order to carry out the assault where you cannot escape, or force you to a roof or basement where you could be in even more danger. Running up and down stairs will get you fit, and is better than taking an unnecessary chance.

- Do not get into a lift with anyone who makes you feel uneasy. Just stand back and look as if you are waiting for someone else. Then use the stairs or wait for the next lift.

- When you get into a lift, check the push buttons to see where the lift is going. If you can tell that it is only going down to the basement – unless that is your destination for, say, the car park – get out. Basements can be dangerous.

- Once in the lift, stand near the controls and face the door. Look at the people coming in so that you give the appearance of being alert and confident.

- If anyone makes you uneasy or bothers you, express your opinion loudly by saying, 'Please stop that,' so that everyone else can hear.

- If you are left on your own in a lift with someone who bothers you or makes you uneasy press all the buttons to ensure the lift stops as soon as possible. Get out and run to the most populated area. Do not hesitate to call out, or leave the building if you can.

Working at home

Take all the standard precautions recommended for safe living at home:

- Use only your initials and surname on your doorbell and in the phone book.
- A Yale-type lock can be easily opened: fit a deadlock to British Standard 3621. Ensure that the door and frame are adequate to withstand assault at these points. Never leave door keys in 'safe' places such as under doormats. Do not give keys to workmen or tradesmen.
- Fit a spyhole or ask any callers to identify themselves.
- Fit a door chain and use it.
- All windows should have locks and these should be secured before you go out. Remember to do the same to accessible ones while you are in.
- Draw curtains or blinds after dark. Do not advertise that you are alone.
- Don't admit anyone unknown without formal identification.
- Should a stranger ask to use your phone, do not let them into the house – offer to make the call yourself.
- If you hear strange noises outside your home, call the police.
- If you lose your keys, change the locks.
- If you go on holiday, cancel the milk and papers. Arrange to have your letters and circulars collected. Inform your Neighbourhood Watch Scheme or at least a trustworthy neighbour.

Working from home
There is a growing army of women who are freelance, self-employed or working from home. Many of these women visit strangers or acquaintances in their own homes. Suzy used to act as a representative for a cosmetics firm. She was paid on commission and she was very ambitious. I am sure in retrospect that she neglected the possible dangers. Be aware of where you are going and check the surroundings and your mode of travel to and from the venue, and be extra careful to follow the previous points.

- Remember that the person should ask for your credentials. Have these ready, introduce yourself, say why you have come and, if appropriate, how long you wish to stay.

- Although your visit may seem to have social overtones, you are in fact at work and should maintain a professional image before your client or interviewee. Be careful to dress and conduct yourself in the way you wish to present yourself.

- If you are at all worried, phone a 'base' number and report where you are and where you are going on to. Make it quite clear that someone is aware of your visit and will be checking on you.

- Do not enter a house at all if the person you had hoped to see is not there – say that you will come back another time. Wait outside in your car if there is only a man by himself who is not the person you have come to see. One woman I know who makes beautiful curtains for a living went to hang them in a house not far from her own. Only the husband was there but he assured her that his wife would soon return from shopping. As she stood on the stepladder reaching up to the bedroom curtain-rail he came up behind her and she was trapped. Knowing that it was only her word against his, and aware that she needed the local business, she kept quiet and suffered privately.

- If you enter an inner-city area which has a high crime rate, proceed with great caution. Ask for police escort if your visit is really necessary. Many GPs, social workers and local council workers are very wary about entering these districts and rarely go alone. I have been amazed, though, at how many female journalists, desperate to be first on a 'story' or determined to prove that a woman can do anything, have plunged into the most dangerous situations without heed, sometimes with very unpleasant results.

- It is essential to leave behind you a record of where you have gone and all your other visits for that day: names, addresses and telephone numbers are all very important. I cannot say it often enough. Do not take your diary with you. LEAVE IT AT HOME and just take the information you need. Arrange for a friend or neighbour to act as 'base' so that you have someone to phone during the day should you need assistance or back-up, and also someone who can 'check you in' when you think you might have a risky day. You could have a reciprocal arrangement. If no one knows where you are, what you are doing and when you are expected home, it will be much longer before anyone starts looking for you should you be in trouble. Working together can decrease individual problems.

One word of reassurance – your chances of being attacked are once in a hundred years! *The average person's chances of becoming a victim are very low.* Some of us have work that forces us to face more problematic situations; all these precautions reduce the risks we take. They are common sense and they are not difficult to follow. I know they are worthwhile for all of us, if only to alleviate the fear of fear.

CHAPTER 5

Aggression

Consultants:

TONY BLACK
Psychologist, Broadmoor Prison Hospital (retired)

STEVIE HOLLAND
Polytechnic of the South Bank

RAY WYRE
Probation officer and police consultant, rape

WOMEN AGAINST SEXUAL HARASSMENT

LYNNE HOWELLS
Training Consultant, Women's Unit, Birmingham City Council

All passages indicated by marginal arrows are directly derived from Jean Orr, 'Managing Aggression', Workbook and Reader for the Distance Learning Centre, Polytechnic of the South Bank, London, 1987, except where otherwise indicated.

Throughout this book we have been thinking together, and I hope learning together, about the ways we can equip ourselves to manage aggression. We have looked at our attitudes and body language, and developed tension control, through which we can defuse aggression. We have worked hard to acquire communication skills which can change aggression to understanding. We have discussed the physical actions we can take to avoid potential aggression and possibly violence. All these techniques and strategies have been related to the workplace or work environment. However, we have not yet actually thought about aggression itself: what it is, why it happens and the behaviour it induces especially in relation to the workplace. Here we will discuss the aggression itself, as well as the potential victim.

This is where the difficulties begin. It is easy enough to describe the physiological changes which take place when a person feels aggressive, but to know how to deal with that aggression in yourself or in another person it is important to understand *why* it happens. There are conflicting theories of aggression, and their essential difference is in the importance given to the role of instinct. In other words, aggression may be:

- an unlearned behaviour pattern which occurs in all mankind whenever there is an adequate stimulus or trigger
- an innate response which is activated by frustration
- a learned behaviour pattern developed from past experiences

I am very much indebted to Stevie Holland and to Lynne Howells once again in this chapter – their work is fascinating.

1 Theories of aggression

Our Trust consultant, Tony Black, who was the psychologist dealing with violent offenders at Broadmoor, guided me through the theories of aggression.

The *instinct theories* put forward by Freud and Lorenz describe aggression as the 'fighting instinct in beast and man which is directed against members of the same species'. Aggression is seen as necessary for the survival of the species because it ensures that the strongest will survive and overcrowding will be avoided.

Most current thinking on the instinct theories certainly favours the idea that there are basic inherent capacities for self-assertion, striving and dominance without which members of the human race could not have survived the struggle for existence. Moreover, these innate drives can be traced to the regions of the brain and nervous system where they have their origins and function. Aggressive behaviour, however, is now thought more likely to be acquired as a result of how our life experiences shape these basic drives for assertion, striving, etc. This explanation also fits better with what is now known of the brain and the nervous system. We therefore find variations of this 'individual–environment' interaction underlying most current instinct theories.

The *frustration theory* considers both events outside ourselves, such as a train being delayed, and internal conflicts between opposing needs. Frustration can have positive effects such as making us redouble our efforts or reassess our goals and abilities. Similarly, experiences other than frustration can lead to aggression, such as incitement, imitation, hostile attitudes and beliefs.

The *frustration/aggression* theory is very convincing especially when the aggression results in violence. Studies have shown that an animal which is frustrated in achieving a particular objective may react by becoming aggressive and direct its energies into violent attacks on the frustrating object. Anyone who has failed to start their car on a cold wet morning will appreciate this. The frustration/aggression theory may be seen in anthropological terms as one of the major explanations of violence in our society today.

Learning theories see aggression as a type of behaviour which, while it is stimulated by underlying drives or urges, is nevertheless mainly learned from past experiences. According to these theories, the individual may respond aggressively if aggression has been successful in satisfying drives and urges in the past. For instance, a child who angrily biffs another when demanding a toy and gets it submissively handed over may continue that behaviour into his working life.

As well as these three main theories, there are other factors to be taken into account – for example, that certain personality character-istics, including a potentiality for violence, can be passed on from parent to child, genetically or by 'modelling' (the child's imitation of parental behaviour and attitudes).

Linked with the genetic theory is the idea that abnormalities may be transmitted by chromosomal sources. In certain males, for example, an extra Y (male) chromosome has been found; these men make up a higher percentage in special security hospitals than within the normal population, though this is still too small a proportion to account for all male violence. But it may be the case that a few violent offenders are the result of chromosomal abnormalities.

The theory of *displacement* may be relevant to some aggressive behaviour, as it suggests that an individual who has been abused by others displaces his violence either on to inanimate objects or on to people over whom he has power or higher status. In this model, aggression is passed from boss to husband to wife to child to cat, or from manager to deputy manager to personal assistant to secretary to client to stranger.

Certain other abnormalities are also linked with aggression. Abnormalities of brain function often follow either illnesses such as meningitis or head injuries. Some kinds of brain damage reduce an individual's ability to inhibit certain behaviour; the behaviour therefore tends to be uncontrolled and, if the individual is angry with other people, there is a greater likelihood of his lashing out violently. This only accounts for a very small number of violent cases in society generally, but it is seen from time to time in hospitals.

The most recent and comprehensive explanations of aggression draw upon all three main theories and their extensions: instinct, frustration and learning based both within the individual and in the environment. The 'social learning model', as it is called, which is used by psychologists such as Bandura, Berkowitz and Buss, incorporates into personality development the influence of instincts and other inherited tendencies, the effect of environment in determining people's needs, values and expectations (as well as what they consider is expected of them), and the strategies people learn for coping with their environment, determined by how successful these strategies have proved to be. It is a complex business mapping out any one person's reasons for being aggressive.

2 The physiology of aggression

The subjective experience of external stress results in arousal of both the emotional and thinking centres of the brain and nervous system. In the newborn child emotional arousal is virtually undifferentiated, that is to say it is either 'on' or 'off' according to circumstance. Fear, pleasure, anger, excitement, rage are all accompanied by a similar arousal. Gradually, as the baby grows, different experiences become associated with the different kinds of occasions when emotional arousal occurs, so we learn to call these arousals fear, pleasure, anger, excitement, rage, etc., as appropriate. Children also develop different ways of dealing with these emotions, and different ways of thinking about them and evaluating their significance, which derive from the various influences, such as instinct and environment, described in the theories above.

The body has a biochemical system which responds to events perceived as stressful, threatening or pleasurably exciting, resulting in the experience of emotions which then serve to prepare the body to perform actions. The 'fright/fight/flight' reaction, for example, encapsulates this sequence. The process is mediated by the release of adrenalin and noradrenalin by the hypothalmus, which is normally under the inhibitory control of the cerebral cortex. Under threat this control is released and the fright/fight/flight response begins. Increased levels of adrenalin and noradrenalin in the blood cause the increase in pulse rate, blood pressure, breathing rate and other physiological changes typical of someone under stress. If the flight is denied or inappropriate, the person may become aggressive and fight instead.

Aggression is behaviour (an 'action' response) inflicting harm (as defined by Buss). It often results from a hostile impulse directed outwards. This can range from an angry look to murder; it can describe a heated argument in which insults are thrown, or physical and emotional violence.

Certain physiological conditions may increase the likelihood of an aggressive outburst, such as hyperactivity of the thyroid gland (thyrotoxicosis) which causes an individual to become over-excited and irritable, epilepsy (particularly of the temporal lobe), and some kinds of brain damage (either temporary or permanent). Agents such as alcohol, other drugs or anaesthesia can also precipitate aggressive behaviour; they appear to lower the individual's level of inhibition, allowing hostile attitudes or other stored resentments to merge more readily into action.

There has also been considerable research into dietary and other metabolic influences upon aggressive or violent behaviour. For instance, it is said that a correlation has been found between the level of sugar intake and delinquent behaviour among young offenders in the USA. Other studies have shown that a society's increase in sugar consumption is paralleled by a rise in violent crime. Food allergies, exercise intolerance and excess lead in the body have all been associated with aggression. Much of this is still disputed but these sources are being increasingly researched.

We are all unique in terms of the blend of inheritance, environment and experience which defines our 'personality'. Often children brought up in the same household are very different, even though they have had similar experiences and share the same parents.

As Jean Orr showed in her work for nurses on dealing with aggression (quoting Smith, 1986, quoting Schauss, 1975), there are many ways that the body's physiological responses to aggression manifest themselves:

Thoughts
Acknowledgement of want or need; misperception: distortion or reality; impaired judgment; diminished concentration

Feelings
Powerlessness; annoyance; anxiety; frustration; resentment; anger; hostility; hurt; humiliation; vengeance; defensiveness; fury; rage

Bodily responses
Increased blood pressure, pulse and respirations; muscle tension; perspiration; flushed skin: nausea, vomiting; dry mouth; yawning; flatulence; itching; blushing; paling; impotence; frigidity

Actions
Direct: Arguing; verbal assaults; blaming others; domineering; demanding; belligerence; manipulation; physical control; combativeness; violence – fighting, rape, homicide, suicide

Indirect: Forgetting; misunderstanding; procrastination; being late; failing to learn

The following list is from the paper written by A. H. Buss in 1971:

Type of aggression	Example
Physical – active – direct	Stabbing, punching, shooting or rape
Physical – active – indirect	Setting a booby trap or hiring an assassin
Physical – passive – direct	Physically preventing an individual from obtaining a desired goal or performing a desired act (as in picketing). Unfair dismissal, withdrawal of touch

Physical – passive – indirect	Refusing to perform necessary tasks (e.g. refusal to move during a sit-in)
Verbal – active – direct	Insulting or derogating another person
Verbal – active – indirect	Spreading malicious rumours or gossip about another individual, belittling capabilities, behaviour, clothes
Verbal – passive – indirect	Refusing to speak or answer questions
Verbal – passive – indirect	Failing to make specific verbal comments (e.g. not speaking up in another person's defence when he or she is unfairly criticized).

3 Dilemmas of aggression

It is plain, if you watch or listen to the news on television or radio, that not all countries have the same attitudes to aggression as we do in the West. Even among the Western countries there are considerable variations in tolerance and response. Some countries have very little aggression indeed. It says something about our society that these are the countries that rarely appear in the media.

Defining aggression is a major problem, since the word covers such a wide range of experiences. Aggression can take many forms, ranging from personal abuse and putting someone down to physical attack and the aggression of war or terrorism. Add to this the fact that we consider aggression legitimate or illegitimate according to circumstances, and the concept becomes all the more complicated.

Today's aggressor may be tomorrow's hero. We have only to read the history books to understand this. When does the freedom fighter become the terrorist? When does the killing glorified in war become unnecessary slaughter? The distinction is not always clear, and it largely depends on who is defining the aggression. We would have a completely different view of our country's history if we studied it abroad.

We use the noun aggression almost always as an expression of disapproval. But we frequently use the adjective as a term of praise when applied to certain people. For example, we talk of aggressive marketing policies, or the aggressive pursuit of reform, or the police aggressively tracking down criminals.

We are trained to see aggression as acceptable in certain situations. It is acceptable to tackle someone on a rugby field but not in a high street. It is acceptable to be verbally aggressive in the House of Commons but not at a social gathering. We might excuse the high spirits of university students but the same behaviour by working-class boys is condemned as vandalism.

Gender makes a difference too. It can be acceptable to call a man aggressive but calling a woman aggressive is a put-down – indeed, an assertive woman is often condemned as aggressive. It is not aggression as such that is frowned upon in our society, but rather who is being aggressive. Culturally, we do not expect women to be aggressive, nor do we consider that people of low status should be aggressive. Aggressive women are 'unladylike' and 'unfeminine'. White middle-class men, on the other hand, are complimented by being called aggressive in business or politics. I would not have believed this if I had not been thrust into the limelight and into a position of talking directly to the professions, industries, civil service and others in a conference or committee situation. The differences are very obvious to a newcomer and occasionally I find them quite disturbing. With some organizations which truly practise equal opportunities I find no problem. With others, I take part in meetings and my points are listened to, but with total incomprehension unless I persist. I have fallen back on the tactic of taking with me a male colleague to reiterate my points. I can literally watch a change in attitude. It often seems such a terrible waste of time.

It is clear that there is wide variation between what different people in different countries, cultures and contexts call 'aggressive'. Yet we have also seen how aggressive behaviour can be quite precisely defined according to the physiological state of the body, following certain experiences perceived as stressful, and in turn followed by quite specific actions.

The following symptoms and signs may indicate the onset of violence:

- agitation and threatening statements or gestures
- clenched fists
- gritting of teeth
- pounding of fists on the table or other objects
- loud, sharp speech

- obvious muscle tension in face, hands and limbs
- high level of activity such as rapid walking, wringing of hands or frequent shifting of position
- inability to cope with stress
- impulsiveness
- paranoid statements
- headaches
- dizziness

It is essential to note the colour of the potential aggressor's face. If someone is pale, he is more dangerous than if he has reddened. Pallor is part of the 'action system' and means that the body is prepared either to fight or to flee. A pale person approaching menacingly really is likely to attack. If, however, he has turned bright red, he is no longer in the initial state of readiness. This sort of person, who will probably explode with roars and curses, may seem alarming, but he is in fact demonstrating that 'his bark is worse than his bite'. But beware of being too complacent! He may revert to pallor and attack.

The media daily use more and more emotive terminology: 'This Means War Says Union Fighter' – you have only to read the sensationalist papers to realize that this way of speaking has spilled over into our daily lives. If for a few days you make an effort to listen to how people talk to one another you will notice how much violence and aggression there is in ordinary conversation. We use many aggressive words ourselves in our daily speech and we are surrounded by violence and aggression in our culture.

This is most evident in films, television and pop music. Many films and television programmes present a picture of life as violent, and it is a violence that costs nothing. Look at the hideous forms of bodily harm that are shown without the characters responsible for them feeling any remorse or compunction, and without any suggestion given that it might hurt to kill or that killing may harm something within the person who does it.

Researchers make connections between American television's widespread dissemination of a violent version of life and the high crime figures. The USA has a homicide rate eight to nine times higher than that of any other major industrial country. However, since Suzy disappeared I have naturally been more sensitive and I now realize that I can watch on British television, almost any night of the week, many ways in which she could have died or suffered.

Pop music often has violent lyrics. The image of pop music, too, can be aggressive – guitars held like guns and singers dressed in leather, chains and studs. Some pop videos show violent scenes such as people being burned or killed. With certain elements in society apparently whipping up and condoning aggressive behaviour, is it surprising that delinquents in the security of an organized group can turn against groups such as the police, who represent authority?

It is perhaps more than time that we sorted ourselves out, stood back objectively and looked at the kind of society we have all been creating and what it has in turn created in us.

4 Coping with aggression within yourself

How well do you think you can handle aggression or cope with the stresses that arouse it? As well as the development and practice of social and interpersonal skills such as those described in this book, much will depend on your attitude, state of physical and emotional health, self-control and past experiences. If you have previously dealt successfully with an aggressive or violent incident you may have more confidence in your ability to handle the problem and will not be panicked into hasty or aggression-provoking behaviour.

When we are confronted with aggression, it is easy to react in an aggressive way. We try to defend ourselves, maintain status or 'get our own back'. The more defensive we are, the more tendency there is to focus on our own feelings and to regard the other person increasingly as a threat.

If you are aware of your own 'natural' feelings in response to hostility directed at you, you will be better able to prevent their intrusion into your relationship with the aggressor. There is nothing shameful in a defensive response to hostility. It merely does nothing to help the aggressor out of his aggression, and it may make things worse for you.

All of us experience a sense of personal frustration at times. We want something badly and circumstances deny it. We ask for a particular day off and are refused. It is part of living in society that we feel a conflict between personal desires and external restraints and prohibitions.

You may experience a considerable degree of frustration and conflict without showing signs of disruptive conduct, but additional tension may result in agitated, emotionally upset behaviour which brings an inability to cope. This is called reaching one's frustration tolerance. Frustration tolerance is not a fixed measure; it varies depending on the situation and the individual. We are able to withstand more tension in some situations than in others. Tolerance will partly depend on what has happened in our recent past and what we anticipate next. Two different people in the same frustrating situation may exhibit a very different frustration tolerance.

If we accept the theory that aggression results, among other things, from frustration, then we could try to reduce the causes of frustration. This is not an easy task, but there are steps we all could take to reduce unnecessary frustration to our colleagues, to clients, and to ourselves. An example of this is the man who has been told that his application for a much-needed grant from the council is under consideration very shortly. What the man has not been told is that this is the first of several committees and departments which will be involved. He has been left in total ignorance of how his request is proceeding and if, indeed, anything is happening at all. Having talked about his frustration with his colleagues, fuelled with their stories of similar experiences, and pushed by his family from behind, he is likely to boil over when met with bland, unhelpful answers from a girl on the desk who will have to make a number of enquiries before she can get the case into perspective. A good briefing, a reasonable and agreed timescale, regular written updates and a well-trained person on the 'frontline' who cares, and who has easy access to information, can avoid, defuse or deal with such problems before they escalate.

Aggression can take a positive form and anger can be a positive emotion. Sometimes they may both be required to ensure a necessary change. It all depends on how we use our anger at injustice in society, and whether we resolve to do something constructive about our feelings, such as joining a pressure group or a political party. If our reaction is negative and anger is expressed in a hostile way, by attacking people or property, our impulses then become destructive.

The most serious forms of violence are preceded by strong feelings of anger. As I have learned from Stevie Holland, angry situations develop through four stages:

- Trigger
- Interpretation
- Arousal
- Behaviour

Stevie uses this illustration:

Imagine a situation where your neighbour plays loud music late at night. You ask yourself – should you (1) discuss it with him over a cup of coffee, (2) play your own music even louder, or (3) bang on his door when this is going on and threaten him?

This is how the row over the noise could have developed.

Trigger You have started a new demanding job and need to get up early.

Interpretation The neighbour knows this and you think he is making a noise on purpose.

Arousal You get really angry one night, your pulse races, you start to sweat and clench your fists.

Behaviour You go up to his door and threaten to hit him or kick the door down.

Result Major confrontation and violent behaviour.

Most people have a wide range of ways in which they handle anger-provoking situations, and have developed coping mechanisms which help to defuse them. So, in the case of the noisy neighbour, instead of confronting him you might invite him in for a cup of tea and chat about the problem or ask him if your music disturbs him. You might on the other hand buy ear plugs, move, or get a night job!

It may be that violent people have not developed such coping mechanisms. They may live a stressful life with a large number of trigger situations. This means that they are on a short fuse and over-react to quite trivial provocations. They may interpret incidents in an exaggerated way and feel that the world is against them, which results in an extreme response.

On the other hand, they may feel angry in a more personal and intimate way on a day-to-day level, with those at work or at home. It is often these small but persistent unsolved problems which lead to an explosion, or to a sense of bitterness in their lives.

If you lose your temper easily and that makes the situation worse, you need to think about why this is and work out ways in which you could change your behaviour. Examine what coping methods you use and decide whether they are short-term or long-term. Look back at the chart on pages 34–35 and see what other methods may be best for you.

If you always or usually tend to employ short-term methods of coping behaviour, your long-term mental health could be damaged.

The long-term methods incorporate constructive realistic ways of coping with anger which can effectively relieve stress for long periods of time. Short-term methods may temporarily reduce anger and tension to a tolerable limit, but they do not deal with the underlying reality.

5 The guises of aggression

VERBAL ABUSE

Asked how they felt about aggression at work, a group of nurses put verbal abuse high on their list of causes of distress. This was reflected in an *Elle* magazine survey inspired by the work of the Suzy Lamplugh Trust. Many of us have been hurt by verbal put-downs such as:

'You are here to do and not to think.'
'That's a stupid remark – is it the best you can do?'

There is considerable aggression in verbal abuse but often it is seen as 'clever' and carries no sanctions. Emotional aggression may develop when workmates or colleagues stop speaking to you, ignore one another, or withdraw their attention.

CONFLICT IN RELATIONSHIPS

Two researchers, Turton and Orr (1985), compiled evidence of why we find violence within families. These are their findings:

Why do we find violence within families?
1 The amount of time spent within the family makes it more likely that violence can occur between members.
2 The activities and interests of the family provide opportunity for conflict; added to this is the overlap or competition of these activities, e.g. what TV programme to watch – or how money should be allocated.
3 Family members have a high level of emotional involvement which can create tensions.
4 There is a presumed right of family members to influence each other and exert control over actions and behaviour.
5 Members represent differing outlooks of age and sex and roles are assigned on these criteria, not on interest or competence.
6 We have a lack of choice in whether we belong to a family. There is limited availability of escape despite divorce.

7 The private nature of families excludes outside contact and makes it easier for violence to take place without censure.

There has been little or no research carried out on this model into the general workplace and environment. However, we might learn some lessons from the points above. Any relationship may have within it a conflict of power. Close personal relationships are very strong; frustration and other provocations for aggression can be subtle but none the less destructive.

MALE–FEMALE CONFLICT

Men often feel a need to assert their authority over women colleagues. Common techniques employed by men in sexual power play include commenting on a woman's attractiveness, and addressing her with familiar endearments such as 'love' or 'dear' in front of male colleagues. A man might also use many words and gestures designed to undermine a woman's power and authority, and subtly diminish her in the eyes of other men.

In order to gain power men may cast business relationships with women in the more familiar social male–female roles. The traditional male roles – father, husband, lover – are useful to men in the workplace because they help men to control women. Men will flirt with female subordinates, for example, in order to make it difficult for them to ask for rises or to refuse to do work that is outside their job description.

If you want to keep your job, you may have to realize that it is no use waiting for men to change their ways or 'see the light'. Your relaxation tension control techniques combined with assertiveness and communication skills should help you to turn the tables gracefully and remind the men that you are a colleague as well as a woman. The following pages might help you too.

One researcher has shown how women are controlled by men through the threat of aggression or violence, be it within the home, on the street or at work. Unfortunately, women who are perceived as aggressive (and this often means that they are being assertive and doing their work well) are subconsciously seen as threatening and may therefore more easily become the victims of aggression. This is certainly not a comfortable notion for either women or men to accept.

6 Sexual harassment

Despite the considerable publicity that sexual harassment has received, it is only recently that employers and trade unions are beginning to provide effective mechanisms for preventing it and for dealing with the problem when it occurs. Much of this success has come about through the hard work of WASH (Women Against Sexual Harassment), whom I asked to help me here.

In many quarters sexual harassment is still seen as a joke. A large number of men are simply ignorant of the effects of their comments. They do not know what is offensive to women or why, nor do they understand that sexual harassment, even in its mildest form, can seem genuinely aggressive to a woman. However, we should remember that what one woman regards as offensive another may find harmless fun. The general rule is that conduct becomes unacceptable when the perpetrator knows – or ought reasonably to know – that it is unwelcome in the circumstances. It therefore follows that every woman should be fully aware of her own level of tolerance and have the confidence and support from her colleagues and employers to draw the line without causing offence or fearing recrimination.

Sexual harassment at work can be divided into six escalating categories:

- *Aesthetic appreciation:* defined as appreciation of physical or sexual features. Remarks such as 'I love that outfit – it really shows your figure.'

- *Active mental groping:* such as men undressing women with their eyes, looking down blouses, etc.

- *Social touching:* apparently within normal conventions but with a caressing hand on the shoulder rather than a friendly hand.

- *Foreplay harassments:* this is when the touching is more openly sexual. Men who consistently brush up against women or who are 'experts' at finding loose hairs on women's clothing or who 'helpfully' tuck in a blouse.

- *Sexual abuse:* this includes verbal abuse, sexual propositions, hugging, kissing, direct touching.

- *Sexual intercourse:* often under the 'ultimate threat' when the victim is told that her career prospect will be jeopardized if she does not consent to sexual relations.

Sexual harassment can make the workplace unpleasant and often intolerable. It is demeaning and undermines confidence, it causes stress and often depression. It can also affect a woman's job performance and may result in her leaving a job rather than continuing to face the harassment. Surveys show that 50–60 per cent of women at work have been sexually harassed. Black women may experience the problem more acutely, since they are often incorrectly believed by white people to be particularly sexually active. Sometimes disabled women find themselves the recipients of unwanted comments and behaviour as well.

There are many reasons why women hesitate to report harassment. Unfortunately, as women are often accused of inviting or provoking the harassment, they do not report abuse because they fear disbelief. Women may also fear that reporting harassment will affect their job prospects and promotion – that they will be ostracized by colleagues of both sexes and laughed at for having no sense of humour. Some women fear publicity and many are not quite sure of themselves, of whether they have indeed 'asked for it' or 'led someone on'. Sometimes women are unsure if what occurred was really sexual harassment.

What do you do if you are being sexually harassed?
First, categorize the man – is he:

- the older man who is just embarrassed by having women around the workplace, especially in authority. This man often makes the kind of comments which might pass for compliments in the social scene but are annoying in the workplace. This kind of colleague is best just accepted, as he is usually fairly harmless.

- the likeable sexist who goes overboard when women are around. This man is likely to call you 'love' or 'dear'. Here you can employ your assertiveness training and just remind him of your name. Repeat it again if he appears not to have heard.

- the man who genuinely likes working with women and does not understand that his mild flirting is offensive. You might find it best to speak to him calmly and directly without rancour.

- one of a group: sexual humour is often used to create group feeling among men. It is usually directed at women to exclude them and give 'the boys' a sense of closeness with each other. Sometimes, however, it is hostile, aggressive humour clearly directed against a woman and the woman's resistance is essential to the joke as it heightens the titillation. Avoid playing them at their own game. It is better just to ignore them and keep out of their way if at all possible. If the situation continues have no hesitation. Go and discuss it with your personnel manager or trade union representative. Take a woman colleague with you if you find it easier.

- a sexist pig or wolf. If a man is being truly obnoxious it will usually be obvious to others. You can ask them to help you if you find the man impossible to ignore. If he assaults you in any way, however, take action straight away. I know that this sounds easier than it may be, for unfortunately the man in question could be your boss or manager or even a client whose account is essential to your firm. It is important to remember (and believe) that no man, whoever he is, has a 'right' to use you as a sexual object. It might be enough to discuss the situation with someone in authority and ask if you can be moved to another department or account. If this fails, talk to the personnel manager or your trade union. Consult wash if you have no representative.

So, if any verbal or physical behaviour makes you feel uncomfortable or distressed at work, you should take a number of steps:

- If you are at all able to use your communication skills, speak up and quite calmly make it clear that you do not like this behaviour. You could do this either verbally or by letter (and do not forget to keep a copy). You could ask a friend to come with you if you need support.

- Talk more openly about the problem, especially to other women in the office. Sharing the experience stops you feeling isolated and enables you to discuss the appropriate action to take.

- Cases of sexual harassment can be difficult to prove. You may find that there are attempts to trivialize the complaint. Keep a record of incidents of harassment, noting the behaviour, time and place of occurrence. This is very important in case a formal action needs to be taken. A well-documented case is crucial. Make sure that your colleagues know that your work is adequate and that they note if the harasser changes his attitude to you in any way.

- Discuss it with senior management or your trade union. I am pleased to say the problem is now beginning to be taken very seriously indeed. If you are self-employed, join a group like WASH.

Facing sexual harassment on your own

There are some odd but surprisingly upsetting incidences of sexual harassment which you usually have to face on your own. One which may seem trite, though it can strike you with particular force, is graffiti, which you may have to pass as you travel to and from work. I am not sure why it seems so personal. It might help to know that you are not alone.

Streakers are usually seen as a joke. However, men with their backs turned, bent over and trousers down are a seriously aggressive signal in such countries as New Zealand. One of my friends had a very unnerving experience. She works from home and had some workmen in to improve her office. After they left she took a film from her camera to be printed, and when she collected the photographs she at first doubted that they were hers – one of the workmen had taken a picture of his fellow builder in this position. The effect was distressing and abusive.

If you have ever seen a flasher you will know that it can feel offensive. Pretending not to see an exhibitionist is the safest reaction. However, do try to look at his face and report him to the police. Flashers can progress to more violent sexual abuse and a profile at the station might come in useful when attempting to track a rapist.

The calmest flasher I ever heard of was one who visited a woman I met when I gave a talk about the Trust. He was her plumber – she came into the kitchen to ask how he was getting on and there he lay under the sink displaying everything. She contemplated asking him to get up and leave immediately but then thought he might as well finish the plumbing first – good plumbers are hard to find! Although she did nothing at the time, she did, I am glad to say, report him to the police. I really admired her remarkably cool reaction, but I always wonder what I would have done in similar circumstances.

7 Assault

You are probably more in danger of rape or assault from men you know than from strangers. As the law stands at the moment, rape is only considered rape if there has been penetration by a penis. Any other form of sexual assault, which might involve broken bottles, knives, sticks, buggery or oral sex, is termed an assault only and carries with it much lower sentences. There is at the moment, I am glad to say, a move within the House of Commons to rectify this anomaly.

In this section I am not being bound by the law. I consider rape to be any assault of a sexual nature, and will discuss that in the pages that follow. Here I want to think about how to recognize, control and deal with an aggressive situation which can and sometimes does lead to violence.

In the first place, it is necessary to recognize that aggressive behaviour may occur in any situation, and naturally it is more important to try to prevent violent behaviour than to worry only about how to manage it when it happens. We must remain aware that every person has the potential to commit violent acts. Usually the strong feelings or emotions which lead to violence are suppressed, contained or sublimated. But each person has his or her own breaking point, when feelings become uncontrollable and must be acted upon.

Where is assault most likely in the workplace?
Assault can of course take place anywhere, but it is likely to be provoked not only by people but also by the environment. Noise, colour, temperature, lack of access to telephones and no clear guidance for visitors can all become stress factors and add to anxiety or tension. To illustrate this think of a waiting room – most emotively, one in a hospital where you are worried about your health – and you will understand how even the most patient of us can reach a breaking point. Boredom, waiting, queue jumping, all increase the tension level: think of buying a stamp at the post office. Working long hours in a hot, noisy environment such as the factory floor can also be fertile ground for a flashpoint.

Think of the opposite picture, an office or workplace that is quiet, cool, decorated with subdued colour and soft lighting, pictures and plants which are visually attractive and relaxing. All these add up to an environment which is non-conducive to aggression.

Who is a possible aggressor?
It could be anyone. You may be attacked not because of who you are but because of what you represent. You may be seen as representing authority, so anger and aggression will be directed at you instead of at

the Housing Department, DHSS, or whatever other branch of the welfare state or commerce has provoked the aggressor. Feelings of resentment are often unleashed on the official who just happens to be there at the time. It might also be that you are simply the 'last straw' in someone's difficult day or life.

When talking to the BMA, for instance, I was horrified by their stories of violence against GPS. One country doctor was called out to a husband whose wife had recently died from breast cancer. When he knocked on the door it opened to reveal the man pointing a shotgun straight at him. The doctor was shot dead. His partner had actually been the doctor dealing with the case.

Obviously it is vital for those who work in the community to understand that they will never know what is behind that door. Social workers, community nurses, home helps, housing officers, estate agents and many others face problems every day. Sometimes it is not only the individual who causes the problem, but a family row. In this case, the worker can often become the focus of everyone's anger and aggression, and be used as a 'conductor' of the violence away from family members.

How do you recognize a possible aggressor?

If you are unaware of the potential for violence, you can be caught unprepared for a violent outburst. Beware of inadvertently becoming the 'trigger' through your words or actions.

One very useful tip. When adrenalin floods the system it makes the hair stand on end. This is very obvious in an animal, but as humans have little body hair there is little visible effect. However, with a shock our short hairs stand on end and we feel the reaction as a creeping sensation on the skin, especially on the back of the neck. Although this may signal nothing to anyone else, it is a sure sign to you yourself that you are in an 'alert' situation. Your instinct is giving you a clear warning that something is wrong. Do not hesitate to take action to minimize the danger.

The advantages of fear

Fear is nothing to be afraid of; many of us feel frightened or nervous at different times. There is a whole range of possible reasons for that fear, but we often have a desire to ignore, suppress or wish away these strong and powerful feelings. However, fear can be a safety mechanism and when acknowledged it can be a source of strength. If we listen to those feelings we are more likely to take control of a situation instead of losing it. We can stop being afraid of our own fear and start using it to our advantage.

Apart from those prickles up the back of the neck, the body has other ways of giving us signals that we are nervous and afraid, some time before it registers in our conscious minds. We must recognize our own particular physical responses to fear so that we can respond quickly. These may include:

Stomach tightening
Stomach churning
Hunched shoulders
Rigid spine
Cold hands and feet
Sweaty palms, forehead, top lip
Jaw tightening
Wobbly legs
Heart beating fast
Breath holding

If you hold your fear inside or pretend it does not exist you ignore a situation which may become very threatening indeed. If you delay action you may become paralysed: you may stop moving, thinking or even breathing. Let your body tremble: any form of action helps to bring out strength and is better than freezing up. It is vital to keep breathing, as breathing keeps the vocal chords open in case you need to shout, and ensures a regular supply of oxygen to the brain so that you can think clearly.

Functions of fear

- The most important function of fear is that *it is information for you to use*. Fear is a better indicator of something threatening than looking for signs of anxiety in others.
- *It signals the possibility of danger.* Stop and assess. It is far better to know what is making you feel frightened than to let those feelings build further.
- *It can be a natural reaction when you are dealing with change or the unknown.*
- *It reminds you that your fears may have come from frightening situations in the past.* Do not ignore them. They have a realistic base.

What to do (in work)
When you are frightened ask yourself:

- Is this person's anger/hostility directed at me, the organization or themselves? Is it a form of distress?
- Am I in danger? If you think you are, leave and get help immediately.
- Am I the best person to deal with this? If you find particular situations difficult, perhaps someone else could handle the situation more effectively. *This is not a cop-out.*

What do you do if you are involved in an aggressive incident?

It is not possible to give rigid guidelines of how to behave but the following pointers may help:

- First of all, never minimize the threat.

- Do not respond aggressively, as this will increase the chance of further aggression. Staying calm is not easy because anger does tend to excite anger in others. Speak gently, slowly and clearly. Do not argue or be enticed into further argument. Do not hide behind your authority, status or jargon such as 'Who do you think you're talking to?' Instead tell them who you are, ask the person's name, and discuss what you want him or her to do. Try to talk things through as reasonable adults (your TA training comes in here) in order to defuse the situation. But always be aware that your first duty is to protect yourself. Remember as an example the incident on pages 58–59.

- Non-verbal communication is equally important – an aggressive stance (such as crossed arms, hands on hips, a wagging finger or a raised arm) will challenge and confront. This is likely to increase aggression. Do not stand too close or above the person. As long as you have ensured you can escape if necessary it is better to sit down and let them stand. Never put a hand on someone who is angry – wait until he or she is completely calm.

- A person on the brink of physical aggression has three possible choices: either to attack, retreat or compromise. Your aim should be to guide them towards the second and third. You can encourage the person to move, to go to the toilet, take a walk round the block, come with you to see another member of staff, etc. You can offer a compromise such as talking through their frustrations or problems, though never offer a promise that you cannot deliver. It is sometimes also possible to divert anger into alternative expression such as banging a table or tearing up paper.

- Trust your own instincts if you feel uneasy. Do not worry about appearing stupid or rude. If the threat of violence is imminent, try to avoid potentially dangerous locations such as tops of staircases, restricted spaces or places where there is furniture or equipment that could be used as a weapon. Keep your eye on potential escape routes; keep yourself between the aggressor and the door. Never turn your back. If you are leaving, move gradually backwards. Ensure that you have the means of escaping from the situation.

- If you are working at someone's home, do not go upstairs or into a back room downstairs, and if at all possible do not enter a house when a man is on his own if you do not know or trust him. Do not hesitate to abandon the visit and arrange to come back at a later date. You can feign illness if necessary to effect an escape. If there is a family argument try to remain neutral and avoid being used by one member of the family to get at the other.

- Never remain alone with an actively violent person; keep a comfortable distance between yourself and the person and do not invade his or her personal space. Keep a desk or other barrier between you and the aggressor. However, be prepared to move; violent people may strike suddenly. Legally, you may only use the minimum reasonable force to restrain someone or you could find yourself charged with assault.

- If no actual assault takes place and you have managed to achieve your objective of calming the situation, effective communication will need to be established or re-established after the violent outburst. This involves setting up a trusting relationship which can only be based on mutual respect. Make a slow gradual approach. Always be aware of the effects of your words and actions and respond accordingly. If you feel it is appropriate you may eventually make a gentle comforting touch. A cup of tea for each of you may cushion the aftershock.

8 Physical attack

Contrary to what people may think, there is no unqualified right to strike an assailant. Self-defence is allowed but only in certain circumstances, and then only if the force used is considered to be reasonable. According to lawyers, redress by way of civil or criminal proceedings is nearly always entirely pointless, while on the other hand the right to use force in self-defence has been considerably eroded. So what actions can you take within the law?

> Where an attack is threatened, the first duty of the potential victim is to retreat. If it is possible to escape, then he/she should do so. It is only when there is no scope for retreating that self-defence should be considered.
>
> There is a statutory right to use reasonable force either to prevent a crime or to apprehend the perpetrator. The definition of reasonable force is not what the victim felt was reasonable in the heat of the moment, but what he/she would have considered reasonable had there been an opportunity for contemplation. While the courts do not press that to ridiculous extremes, they do expect people not to over-react and to try and assess the actual threat posed.
>
> If the attacker is unarmed, and obviously of a weak physical disposition, it would not be held reasonable to inflict injuries upon him that were far more severe than could possibly be necessary to fend off the attack. The use of any weapon might well be considered unnecessary.
>
> But on the other hand, where the attacker is armed, and is in a position to do a lot of damage, a degree of force sufficient to halt him, even if it entails rendering him unconscious or inflicting grave injury, will almost certainly be justified. No more force than is necessary should be used. [Andrew Martin, *The Case for Self-Defence* (1978)]

The problem is, of course, that it is extremely difficult to indulge in that degree of objectivity which the law requires. The more dangerous the situation, the harder it will be to form an accurate opinion as to the relative risks.

I myself think it is much more helpful to remember that it is the offender who is responsible. It is not your fault, you are not to blame, and this is the time when you have those three options to choose from:

attack
flight
compromise

It is safer for you, too, to choose either of the last two.

Flight

Get away as fast as you can. Do not stop to think. Act. Run away, preferably towards a place where you know there will be people. It is always better to run if you can rather than stay and confront an attacker.

Compromise

Yell, scream, grab your awareness alarm and set it off by your aggressor's ear or better still throw it out of reach (if it's one of those alarms which stays activated when pressed). He will have to choose between you and the deafening noise it will be making. Practise yelling and screaming. It takes confidence and relaxation –beware of crying wolf. Make sure you are out of earshot during your practice sessions!

How do you make sure you can yell, shout or scream especially under stress or terror? The first thing to remember is that there is only one way to open your mouth really wide. Open your mouth as wide as you can and then look at yourself in a mirror. If you have raised your upper lip high you will find that it is almost impossible to let out a loud sound. There is a very simple reason for this, discovered by Mr Alexander, the pioneer of the Alexander Technique, a Tasmanian actor who kept losing his voice. One day he caught sight of himself in a mirror and he noticed the way he held his head and used his jaw. Going back to the skeleton it was not hard to see that the windpipe was unable to work properly if the head was tilted back and the lips raised. The only way you can efficiently open your mouth widely is to drop the lower jaw. If you put your index finger on either side of your face just below the lobe of the ear you will find the joint of the jaw. Now relax the jaw muscles and you are ready. First, expel all the air you can until you feel your tummy tighten, now relax and allow the air to fill the vacuum. Then expel all the air with a rush and a yell/shout and you will surprise even yourself. If necessary clasp both hands on your diaphragm and push. This might well break through an immobile 'freeze' of panic.

Attack

If you cannot run away and your instinct is that fighting back might work, then fight with as much anger as you can and without constraint. I still meet many people who say, 'Oh, I couldn't hurt him. After all he's somebody's son.' Remember this is your life and it is worth fighting for: claw at his face, go for his windpipe, go for wherever it may hurt. Do not worry about hurting your attacker: you must get free.

(1) Try to make the knee your first target – it is the weakest joint and when struck or kicked properly it is totally disabled. Remember that when your kick lands your knee must still be bent. Aim to kick *through* not at the knee.

(2) The solar plexus is a vital striking area. It is the centre of a web of nerves and a forceful flow with an elbow, umbrella or walking stick has a paralysing effect. The attacker will feel a deep sense of nausea so intense that even a drunkard or a person high on drugs can be stopped.

(3) The elbow joint is also very weak. Strike the elbow joint with the palm of your hand when the attacker's arm is straight. At the same time, jerk his wrist against the pressure. It is very painful and disabling.

(4) Under the armpit, slightly to the front, is a very vulnerable spot. It is an area rich in nerves and arteries and a walking stick, umbrella point, key or ballpoint pen jabbed here causes intense pain.

(5) The large area running down the side of the rib cage. Any blow here can be painful. A palm or heel, a bunch of keys, a pencil or pen, stick or umbrella, even a hardback book, especially if the strike is hard, will cause great pain.

(6) The shin bone is another prime target. A vicious kick with the inside of your shoe will cause intense pain, even more if you can scrape the edge of your shoe down the shin and stamp on the arch of the foot. Beware of the vulnerability of standing on one leg and be sure you can get away.

(7) The face: dig in deep under the cheekbone with your thumbs, pencil or key and at the same time push upwards. Try twisting the ears off or shout down them; slap both sides of the head. A sharp quick strike between the eyes can knock your attacker unconscious. If your life is in danger, strike hard.

(8) The fingers. Bend any finger right back (not just a little way). Stamp on them, bite them, pull them apart. A broken finger is completely disabling.

Do not try aiming at his eyes with your fingers. Most of us find that psychologically impossible and you may draw back at the vital moment and find yourself in an even more vulnerable position. Also avoid trying to knee your attacker in the groin or testicles. This area is usually far too high to be able to reach easily and men are naturally very protective of this part of their body. And if you miss you will be left in a highly vulnerable position in which you can easily be pushed over flat on your back.

All you need to do is disable your attacker and then leave the scene. If you do manage to free yourself, run away immediately. Do not stop to have one more go at him or to see what you have done. The idea is to 'bash' and 'dash'!

Self-defence

Self-defence classes are now increasingly available. They are organized by women's groups, police volunteers, youth clubs, residents' associations and adult education centres. At the moment many of these classes are taught by people who are in fact not teachers at all but merely members of some form of martial art. There should be some safety guidelines for the teaching of self-defence to women, to make classes safer in themselves. It is essential that all guidelines should be kept to a minimum and be simple to learn. However, it is wise to remember:

- Self-defence will not turn you into a person who does not have to avoid risks. There are some dangerous situations (such as being attacked by several people or with a gun or knife) that even a martial-arts expert could not handle.

- Besides being well taught, self-defence techniques need to be practised regularly. It is no good going to a few classes and thinking that for the rest of your life you will be able to defend yourself. If they are not practised your skills will fade.

- However much self-defence training you may have had, there are always times when you are not on top form, tired or ill.

- Self-defence techniques should not be tested out unnecessarily. Do not walk deliberately into trouble as an experiment. In any violent physical contact, everyone will be hurt.

- There are only a few physical self-defence moves which can be taught safely in a book. Most need to be taught and practised in a class. You need 'hands-on' physical practice with a teacher in whom you have confidence, but not so much practice that you think you do not have to take care.

9 Rape

Rape is a life-threatening situation, and violence or the threat of violence seems to present an 'all-or-nothing' option. For this section I consulted Mary-Helen Dewar, who was a nurse and health visitor. She now works in stress management and is a JP. I have also consulted Ray Wyre, who is one of the foremost experts on rape in Great Britain. His book *Women, Men and Rape* is one of the most sensible, balanced and helpful works I have read. Ray believes with me that physical self-defence training can create a false sense of security which may collapse in the event of a violent attack and leave the victim otherwise unprepared.

Many victims actually freeze with fear and often put up little resistance. This is unfortunately often taken by the rapist to signify assent and by the police and courts to show that the woman had acquiesced and that therefore rape had not technically taken place. This is, of course, nonsense. Not fighting back physically does not mean not resisting attack.

There are, however, several steps that you can take to help yourself. Let us look first at the various kinds of sex offender that have been identified by Ray Wyre. Each one may respond to a different approach.

- *The sexual rapist:* he usually lacks social skills and appears passive and submissive. He has a poor self-image, and finds it difficult to start conversations. He has unusually strong sexual urges which he feels he can only satisfy through attack.

    These men have a history of petty sex offences, obscene phone calls, indecent exposure and minor sexual assault. They will use just enough force to commit the act and their fantasy is that their victims will respond to their attack by submitting willingly. Sexual rapists in particular say that they have gone through with rape attacks because they met with little or no verbal protest. The sexual rapist will jump out, making a grab at his victim, saying nothing or simply threatening her. They are the most likely to back off if they meet verbal or physical resistance.

- *The anger rapist:* he is usually a man with a dominant woman – mother, girlfriend or wife – in his life. His style is macho. He may be attractive and have social graces but he will become enraged if his masculinity is questioned. He often feels put down and dominated by women and either puts them on a pedestal or sees them as unfaithful and hostile. He deflects his anger on to unsuspecting women and his aim is to dominate, degrade and control. Because his attacks are often related to a breakdown in an existing relationship, he is likely to attack a stranger within a few miles of his home. The anger rapist tends to be demonstratively angry, using abusive language and violence. Physical resistance is likely to make him worse. Try all your communication skills – talk, talk, talk, and do whatever seems best to stay alive: urinating, fainting, epileptic-type fits may all be effective non-provoking forms of resistance.

- *The sadistic rapist:* he is rare and the most dangerous. He may use an implement in his sexual attack and take his victims to a safe area where he can keep them for several hours.

  There are different types. Some will be aggressive in social situations and will express the idea that women like being knocked about. Others are over-controlled and have a strong religious background. They will regard themselves as punishing their victims for having made them sin. Their turn-on is their victim's fear and pain. Keep calm and constantly look for moments when you could make a sudden move to escape. Do not try physical resistance.

- *The sociopathic rapist:* this man is primarily a criminal who begins to rape while committing other crimes, such as housebreaking. He may go on to pick up women to rape them and most of his attacks occur in the homes of his victims or in his own home. He is selfish and sees rape as just another form of anti-social behaviour. He uses minimal violence and though he may produce a weapon, he is unlikely to use it. He is concerned not to be caught and develops strategies that make conviction difficult. The sociopathic rapist will use social skills to engage his victim in what looks like the promise of a relationship. Beware of the salesman who asks for a date, the man who asks for a drink after work and then wants to take you back to 'look at his pictures'. This is the type of rape scene which can leave you feeling more guilty for having 'asked for it', or 'I should have seen it happening', etc. Do not allow one-night stands or take up offers from strangers. With this type of rapist first try assertiveness, then try talking to him person-to-person before trying any physical tactics – that is if you have not had the sense to get away quickly when you instinctively felt that his approach was 'wrong'.

It is important to remember that most rapes occur within a relationship – a date relationship; an employer–employee or professional–client relationship. Unless you are very unlucky and have struck up a friendship with a sadist (and you may be able to recognize them from the description above) it is unlikely that you will be having a relationship with a rapist, either a sexual rapist who finds it difficult to relate socially, or an anger rapist, whose victims are usually strangers. These are the two kinds of people by whom you might be attacked going to and from your workplace, and because of whom it is wise to take the avoidance procedures discussed in Chapter 3. It is the sociopathic rapist who might fool you in the work situation.

These men can be very charming, but they are also very cunning. The sociopathic rapist likes to parade his woman, and thinks of himself as masterful; you will have to do what he wants and go where he wishes but when he is with his mates he will ignore you completely. He will needle a woman until she feels angry but will still insist or force her to have sex with him. Through a blend of bullying, persistence and brute strength he will get his way. He may not even consider this rape. There are, of course, many variations, but this is the most difficult rapist to detect or convict. Of course, the type shades off into a common or so-called 'normal' type of male in our society.

Any sexual act which is forced upon you without your consent is rape, even if you know the man or he is your husband. Ray Wyre's six phases might help you learn to anticipate, negotiate and eventually gain control in a rape situation. Each of them offers an opportunity for action, however limited, which might change the rapist's course or at least restrict the physical or psychological damage you will suffer.

Phase one – planning the attack
Sexual attacks may seem spontaneous, but most are carefully planned and rely on the victim's lack of caution. Sexual offenders fantasize frequently about their attacks, sometimes for months ahead. They look for areas where there is least chance of interruption, where they can take their victims or where women sometimes go alone. Most favour a time and place where there is limited light. They often pick on a type of woman, possibly one who looks vulnerable, and will let others pass. You can reduce your chances of becoming a victim by following the avoidance strategies in Chapter 4.

Phase two – the approach

The main safety suggestion at this stage is to act on your intuition. If you feel any misgiving about an approach, turn and walk firmly towards a more populated area. Do not worry about whether you are giving offence. Women are socialized to be helpful and inoffensive, and rapists will take advantage of this.

If you are followed, don't walk faster – a gradual speeding up can excite rapists. Just keep going and then break into a run when you can: if you are still being pursued, don't shout 'Rape'. Shout 'Fire'; yell 'phone the police' – people are more likely to respond if they don't anticipate violence. Act on your intuition.

Phase three – the initial attack

You may be attacked physically or restrained and threatened with the consequences if you don't do as you are told. An order like 'Do as I tell you or I'll destroy your face', though very frightening, does not forbid you to speak. Try responding verbally in a clear, firm and unequivocal way, using assertive language. Make it clear that in no way will you permit sexual contact. 'Don't touch me', 'Please keep your distance', 'I won't have sex', 'Leave me alone', 'Go away', 'I'm a virgin'. If your assailant is a sexual rapist such a response may make you an inappropriate target according to his plan. At this point follow your instincts – check out how you measure up to your attacker psychologically. You may still have a chance to run. Be assertive.

Phase four – person to person

If assertiveness fails, switch your approach. Try empathy towards your attacker. In his head, and probably in other attacks, he has rehearsed what is happening. You are trying to deny the fantasy role he has chosen for you. Your aim is to break through this fantasy until he fully understands that you are a real person.

Your best hope of survival could be in building a relationship with your attacker. Give him your first name. Ask him about himself, about the problems he must be facing to behave as he is, problems about women, bad past experiences. You might talk about his feelings of rejection or his frustration that he has been unable to control his behaviour. Stop talking only if he threatens to hurt you if you do not. The longer he lets you talk the more likely you are to succeed in ending the attack. If you have to be quiet, listen to him, respond with understanding. This will reduce your anxiety too, so you can think more clearly. Remember, you may be terrified, but the rapist may well be frightened too. Even if you do not avoid rape, you may reduce any further violence against you.

If empathy fails, try eliciting sympathy. Tell him truth or lies about menstruation (it puts some men off), being pregnant, gynaecological infections, venereal disease, mental illness, bereavement – such things may disqualify you as an object of his fantasies. In the last resort, buy time – someone may come along. Give empathy and sympathy every chance.

Phase five – the attack

Your attacker will attempt to get you to be an active partner by threats or by physically forcing you, with varying degrees of violence, to do what he wants. You have to rely on your instincts. Though difficult, expressing the wish to take the more dominant role may reduce injury.

The amount of resistance a woman offers will be determined by the degree of violence used against her and her response to a life-threatening situation. Do whatever seems best to stay alive. Urinating, fainting, and epileptic-type fits may be effective non-provoking forms of resistance. Putting up a struggle may excite some attackers and cause premature ejaculation, but it may also provoke more violence. In any event make sure that you scratch him, as it is now possible to prove identity from the genetic 'fingerprinting' which can be traced from even minute particles of tissue and blood left under the fingernails. If you intend to use violence you should probably do so early in the attack. But choose a moment of maximum surprise, lull your attacker into a false sense of security, and then use the violence to give yourself a chance to run away.

Try to notice as much as you can about your attacker: his appearance, his words and actions. The police will ask you some very specific questions, which are outlined below.

Phase six – after the assault

The rape has taken place but you are still in danger. Your attacker is deciding how to leave you. He may threaten to harm you or your children if you report the attack. He may apologize and make a bargain with you. Tell him you couldn't face telling anyone about what happened. Reassure him. If he offers to let you go, accept immediately. Some rapists have almost given their victims a chance to escape by leaving them unattended for a time. It is usually women too frightened to move who have in consequence suffered a physical attack or a second sexual attack when they might have got away. Walk, run, leave the scene as soon as you get a chance.

Phase seven
Finally, talk about the attack to someone, otherwise you may have to live with the psychological consequences for years. Talk to Rape Crisis and to people close to you who will help you deal with the legacy of fear, guilt, self-blame and loss of self-respect a rape victim is left with.

Many women do not report rape to the police, for reasons which have been well documented. But, as a consequence, their attackers go on to rape other women. Convicted rapists have confessed to many offences of which they have never been accused. For the sake of others, have the courage to go to the police. This will lead to more arrests and greater emphasis on reform.

When you do go to the police, go as soon as you can. You will need all the self-control that you can muster. You may feel in need of alcohol or be offered a tranquillizer. Do not take either, as you will need to give a clear account of what happened. Also, however difficult or unpleasant it is, resist the immediate need to wash or change your clothing: you will be removing vital evidence. Do not clean your fingernails either, because if you have managed to scratch the attacker you will be carrying identifying evidence of blood and skin.

Try to remember everything you can about your attacker:

- Have you seen him before?
- How old was he?
- Height and build?
- Complexion/skin colour?
- Shape of face, clean-shaven or bearded?
- Colour of eyes?
- Type of clothing?
- Any distinguishing gestures or features, tattoos, scars or jewellery?
- Voice: did he have an accent?
- Did he have a vehicle – can you describe it?
- Did you see which way he went?

Remember, the police are trying to build up a full picture of your attacker and they will need to have your further observations.
Sexual activity: It is important to note the order in which your

attacker told or asked you to do things. They will want to know the manner he used: was he rough or gentle, was there a sequence or pattern? Did he want sex orally (using your mouth), vaginally (your front passage) or anally (your back passage), or did he want a combination? Did he want to kiss you or you to kiss him? Did he ask you to do certain things to 'turn him on' and if so, what? Did he keep saying he wanted you to 'enjoy it'? All these points are vital in helping the police in their efforts to find the rapist and prevent further harm to others.

SUPPORT AND COUNSELLING

Your first reaction may be to keep quiet and try to cope alone. However, it seems that if you can talk about what has happened and 'relive' the rape after the incident you may in fact feel calmer, more in control and less stressed. It can be very therapeutic to talk to an appropriately trained counsellor after a rape. This will give you an opportunity to talk about yourself and to make choices for your 'life after rape' which might help you to recover more fully. With trained counselling you will gradually feel better and gain confidence, and coping will be easier.

Attitudes and procedures have changed for the better during the last few years. The police are being trained to work sensitively with rape victims to help with their situation, feelings and reporting. You will probably receive some on-the-spot support and counselling from the police themselves. They or the Citizens Advice Bureau can put you in touch with appropriate counsellors and counselling agencies for more long-term help. Some GPs have counsellors working from their own surgeries. Some firms have counsellors on the staff, or employ independent professional counselling services to aid staff welfare.

There may be self-help groups in your vicinity. There may be a local Well Women's Centre. Some of this help is free; some ask for a minimal fee. There may be stress-management courses which you could attend. Remember to use all the tension control techniques in this book. Do not neglect exercise, especially walking, cycling and swimming. Develop an interest which you really enjoy. All this raises your self-respect.

Social support is also the key to your future well-being, to help you regain your balance in life. Even if you don't want to tell your family and friends, think about letting them help you through 'a difficult time'. They will probably notice that you are not quite yourself. They do not have to know exactly what happened, but they may well give you support and encouragement in the absence of information. Gradually, as you feel more confident, you may be able to talk to them about what happened.

Always carry with you the absolute conviction that rape, whether it is attempted or actual, is NOT YOUR FAULT – no one should ever be raped!

CHAPTER 6

Action

Consultants:

LYNNE HOWELLS
Training Consultant, Women's Unit, Birmingham City Council

TRADES UNION CONGRESS

DEPARTMENT OF HEALTH AND SOCIAL SECURITY

CAMBRIDGE COUNTY COUNCIL

WANDSWORTH BOROUGH COUNCIL

Researching material for this last chapter has been a mammoth task which I could not possibly have completed without the help of Lynne Howells, Cambridge County Council and Wandsworth Borough Council. Indeed it struck me forcibly as I waded through material sent to me by the TUC, the DHSS and others that although there has been a great deal written and, as far as I can see, hundreds of hours spent talking and considering, in fact there has been very little action. Having considered all the facts – and they are facts – very seriously and I hope objectively, I find this lack of action very hard to understand.

Sociologically, the female is seen to be the 'carer'. It is therefore hardly surprising that the majority of research into violence at work has been into the caring professions – social work, nursing, etc. Human 'carers' are *the* essential part of the services and ought to be a priority to their employers. So why do they remain so unprotected?

Commercially, this reaction does not make sense either. Companies go to great lengths to protect their money, their production and their products, but without their trained personnel they would be undermined. Staff who are in fear, harassed or working in actual or potentially aggressive situations are unlikely to work effectively or efficiently. They are also more likely to be absent through stress-related illness. When a company invests money in training and keeping staff, staff becomes an asset entitled to equal protection. But for some reason there are company managers who have not yet reached this conclusion.

So far this book has been about how individual women can take the initiative to protect themselves against aggression in the workplace. However, it cannot be stressed too strongly that aggression is not solely the woman's problem but society's too. It is vital that employers, managers and those in authority take responsibility for their own lack of action. While women *can* help themselves, I want to advocate here that the individual woman joins with another individual and with another so that eventually they form pressure groups for action in the workplace, outside the workplace, anywhere that two or three women are gathered together. It is essential that they should have the support of men. I see this as a chance for women to gain confidence about themselves and for men to come to terms with and value this confidence. This means employers working with employees, management working with trade unions, and government, all sides of the House and the Establishment being involved. Society's problems need to be solved by society, and that means everyone.

1 The role of management

What part do we want management to play in our quest to beat aggression? It might help to look at some examples. The first comes from a letter which we printed in our second edition of *The Acorn*, the Suzy Lamplugh Trust magazine:

> 'I work as an estate officer for a local authority. This used to be a male domain but slowly women are entering the profession. The job involves visiting clients in their homes and dealing with their housing and related problems. Often the people I visit may not want to see me, may be disturbed, mentally ill or violent, but I would not know this beforehand.
>
> We arrange our own appointments and are out of the office all day from 10 am to 4 pm, so it would be a long time before I was missed, and no one would have a clue where I was if I went missing. I feel very vulnerable but find this difficult to express to my colleagues (five male, one female). I asked if we could all do a self-defence course, but my colleagues and senior officers laughed. They said if I couldn't talk my way out of a situation then I shouldn't be doing the job. I've done it for eight years now! I am expected to be a woman and not lose my femininity, but if I ask for help, it is suggested that as a woman I can't do the job. Even the men pair up for some jobs but they have made it so that I won't even ask for help now. The other woman in the office seems totally unafraid and does not support me.
>
> If, in my private life, I put myself into the situations that my work demands, people would think I was mad and asking to be attacked.'

In this case, the estate officer has recognized that there is a genuine problem. She has come into conflict with and suffered verbal abuse from her colleagues and she is totally unsupported by the local authority, who seem to have neglected the facts that personnel are no longer solely male, and that everyone within this team needs support. There is an unspoken agreement between some team members to cover each other, but only at the cost of not admitting fear. I believe that employers have a responsibility for the safety of their staff and that, male or female, there should be procedures to ensure that employees do not walk unprotected into a dangerous situation. The first move by the estate officer could be to approach her trade union, who would most probably take up these points with the Local Authority.

The next example reached the Industrial Tribunal.

Every year, a certain firm of accountants visited a firm in the north to undertake their audit. Each year Mrs B., the chairman's personal assistant, dreaded the arrival of one of the team who always made a beeline for her, teasing her, touching her up and then, aroused by her discomfort, making her life very unpleasant. She had never told her boss, but it certainly affected her work. This time he was as bad as ever. Early one evening she escaped with her colleagues, to whom she told all her feelings as she relaxed in the pub. She was disconcerted when her tormentor followed them there and joined them at their table. Surrounded by her friends and emboldened by the alcohol, when he once more made a 'pass' she picked up her glass of beer and poured it all over his head. The accountant left immediately and Mrs B. felt relieved but slightly embarrassed. When she got to work the next day she received her notice. Her case took eighteen months to come up, by which time she had lost her nerve and energy and was unemployable.

This was, of course, a culmination of mistakes. Mrs B. could have been trained in tension control, body language and assertion techniques. These skills would have helped her to make her feelings clear to the accountant without too much distress to either party. But it is essential for management to acknowledge that, in most cases, involvement in aggression within the office should not reflect adversely on staff or be viewed as poor practice. Mrs B., though she reacted in a way which aggravated the situation, was not to blame for the situation arising in the first place. Staff training combined with good office procedure encourages open communication, which might in this case have saved embarrassment, ill feeling, a lost career and upheaval in the office.

A third example involved a woman employer.

Jenny had been taken on as a trainee under a well-known and talented interior designer. She had been with the firm six months and was just twenty years old. She still lived at home as her pay was low and so far she had not progressed beyond the shop. She had made no consultation 'outcalls' and looked forward to that progression. Out of the blue she was asked by her boss to go up to Huddersfield the following Monday to do an 'outcall' on an unknown client who would meet her at the station. Because Jenny had known my daughter, Suzy, by sight and she herself had had three unfortunate experiences when travelling by train, she was wary. She said she would certainly go, but only if accompanied by another trainee. Her employer was very angry, told her that she was weedy, would never get anywhere and was not fit for employment. Jenny stood her ground. The deputy director eventually went to Huddersfield instead; Jenny's relationship with her boss was weakened and she left as soon as possible to join her mother's shop. Everyone lost out.

Every woman who embarks on a career should be aware of the kind of work it entails and be prepared to do it to the best of her ability, even if it involves some difficult situations. That said, however, she should also be fully trained and equipped to face any problems, and Jenny quite obviously had not reached this stage. The employer must accept the responsibility for reducing risks to staff (sometimes it is not possible to eliminate them), introducing preventive and protective measures and issuing clear policies and procedures. These would include taking account of an instinctive reaction from an employee to a potentially problematic situation. It is a temptation for battle-emboldened survivors to expect others to survive the tests of the workplace without realizing that experience can come too late. Suzy's abduction brought to the surface a realization of the often unknown hazards and dangers. Today's women need to be trained in awareness, and equipped with the knowledge of how to thrive.

2 The way ahead

How can we, as individuals, together with other individuals, encourage all-round involvement in beating aggression? In the first place, we can raise awareness of the problem.

RECOGNITION

At present, very few organizations keep statistics on the problem of aggression. The research which has been set up by the Suzy Lamplugh Trust at the London School of Economics on the Changing Workplace should prove a major contribution in this field. Staff often feel that aggression and violence are an unavoidable if unpleasant part of their job. They are rarely motivated to fill in incident forms unless there has been a physical injury which requires time off. A very recent survey (1987) carried out by the Health Services Advisory Committee in five health authorities found that out of 3000 completed questionnaires, 1 in 200 (0.5 per cent) had suffered an injury requiring medical assistance during the previous twelve months, more than 1 in 10 (11 per cent) had sustained minor injuries, 1 in 21 (4.6 per cent) had been threatened with a weapon, and more than 1 in 6 (17.5 per cent) had been threatened verbally. Similar surveys have shown that the average social worker can expect to be attacked once a year.

Dealing with aggression is about establishing good working practices. It will help everyone if issues that regularly and consistently affect employees are dealt with in an open and positive way. Anyone who has had the opportunity to discuss aggression at work says that being able to talk about incidents openly can alleviate the problem, as long as the discussion is taken seriously. We can start by talking among ourselves and drawing in others so that more people become aware of this previously hidden issue.

IDENTIFICATION

Naturally, nearly every workplace and type of work will have its own needs and problems. However, most managements tend to relate violence and aggression at work to incidents where a customer lashes out at a member of staff in an unpredictable way. These incidents are therefore seen as 'one-off' and considered in isolation.

Employees would probably find a broader base to the problem – including sexual harassment and racism, even culture and class bias. Aggression from colleagues, which can be least expected, can be hardest to cope with, and certainly more frustrating than aggression coming from outside. To have the confidence to deal effectively with customers, clients or the public, you need to know you have the necessary support on home ground, instead of finding yourself undermined by additional, unnecessary hazards.

Nor do most women employees see the problem of aggression as shared equally with their male colleagues. This is not solely because women fear aggression and are affected by it more than men. It may be simply because of the different kinds of job that women and men tend to do. The majority of employees who deal with the public, both in the public and private sector, are women.

In all organizations where staff deal directly with the public, the potential for violence is there. Clearly the employer cannot guard against all eventualities, but the way in which jobs are designed and performed can affect the occurrence of violence. The public sector, particularly, is having increasing difficulty in providing services adequate to meet the public need. Tensions occur as front-line staff bear the immediate responsibility for explaining cutbacks, policies and procedures to the public, and they take the brunt of decisions over which they have had little control.

In both the public and the private sector, the commitment of staff to a customer-centred approach will often depend on their own feelings of job satisfaction and security, which in turn will depend to some extent on staffing levels, hours of work, level of managerial support and other factors. Customers can easily feel uncared for and frustrated by what they see as unhelpful bureaucratic systems and procedures. Ignoring the problems this creates – which are essentially management issues – leads to subordinate staff being unable to cope, then becoming ill and eventually leaving.

This issue must be brought to wide attention so that management understand that the way staff are treated and the protection available are crucial not only for safety, but also for maximum efficiency and effectiveness.

ACTUALITY

When we have succeeded in recognizing and identifying the problem of aggression within our own particular workplace, the next step is to persuade management to initiate data collection to establish the actuality. One of the most regular failings of management, when thinking about prevention, is to introduce measures on the basis of an assumed definition of the problem or because an organization needs to be seen to be 'doing something' immediately. Difficulties will arise or dictates will simply be dismissed as irrelevant, when they are issued from the top – from high-level management as much as from a parent or professional body – without making allowance for differing local experiences and without any reference to the specific needs of employees.

Probably the most reliable base from which to start is to:

- create an atmosphere and procedure at work where discussing fear and other problems is not a mark of failure but is seen as part of good practice.

- accept that the employer has a responsibility to provide direction and support for his employees, and that all employees have an individual responsibility never to put themselves, their colleagues, clients or members of the public at unnecessary risk.

- formulate a simple and effective recording system which meets the need of the organization. The system must be able to record the whole range of situations from physical violence to verbal abuse, from sexual harassment to rape, from innuendo to assault. This should have three functions:
  1 To collect statistical data on the number and types of incidents for both legal and financial reasons.
  2 To contain enough information to analyse incidents to see where improvements could be made and lessons learned.
  3 To be part of the monitoring process which will adapt and change organizational policy where necessary.

Unless the climate for discussing these issues and a formal system for recording incidents exist alongside each other, the whole problem can easily remain at a mythical level and the responses from both employees and management will be totally inappropriate. It is not until a rounded view of what is happening within a particular workplace has been obtained that it is possible to see the reality. It will then be possible to pull out the common threads running through particular incidents. Unless this is done systematically, even simple changes cannot be made, or changes will be made which are difficult to put into practice. Armed with this information, it will be possible to search for preventive measures that are likely to be helpful and achievable.

PREVENTIVE MEASURES

With the benefit of the facts, employers should then consult with their employees to see what changes need to be made.

Some suggestions may be costly, such as increased staffing levels, separate reception/office/switchboard duties, training for everyone. Some will highlight what should be happening but is not, such as increased management support, good induction programmes, proper diary systems, accurate information on customers, or a planned policy for dealing with difficult customers. Others will indicate the need for policy decisions such as guidelines, an equal opportunities policy, a statement of commitment to employees, advertising the customer's right to complain, or better relations with the media.

First of all it is important to evaluate all preventive measures which could make the working environment healthier for employees and customers alike. The next stage should be to estimate whether these measures are financially viable. So, having gained a full picture of the problem and some of the measures which will ease it, it is then possible to plan the overall strategy.

Of course, decisions will need to be taken on priorities, cost, timescale implementation and monitoring. Remember, it is often easier to introduce immediate stopgap measures in response to pressure from employees, public concern or simply because they seem inexpensive. Some may be appropriate, but many are likely to be ineffective if not carefully thought through.

It is necessary to consider the acceptability of measures to both customers and employees. Some banks, for instance, are now returning to a situation where transactions are made without barriers, to encourage better relations between staff and customers. Other organizations consider nailing down furniture and putting up screens to be essential safety measures. Decisions must be appropriate to the philosophy of the organization as a whole.

THE OVERALL STRATEGY

Now will be the time for management and employees to consult together and decide which preventive measures will best suit their own needs and workplace. The following list might be helpful in setting an agenda. Many of the points will be useful, others may not apply; some firms will already cover most of these points; but everyone benefits from a re-evaluation of the rules.

Policy

Commitment from the employer to support employees who are subject to aggressive behaviour in the course of their employment. The extent of this support should be determined according to the individual circumstances of each incident. Legal advice should normally be available from a solicitor when necessary and a personal accident assault risk policy be held to cover violent and criminal assault. In the event of any employee believing that he or she has incurred loss which falls outside the insurance policy, an independent assessor could be appointed to determine whether compensation should be paid.

Every incident of actual or threatened aggression should be reported on an appropriate form. If a first-aid book is kept already, perhaps the reporting should be coordinated to save extra paperwork and ensure cross-referencing. Each incident, however trivial it may seem, should be investigated by an appointed person and the report made and processed according to agreed procedures. An index of these incidents should be made for monitoring and evaluation so that a report can be sent to an authorized person or committee.

Guidelines Given the special requirements of the individual workplace and employment, guidelines should be drawn up which provide staff at all levels with clear direction on the most effective ways of preventing aggressive behaviour, and on how to protect those people involved from its consequences. It should also be recognized that guidelines can never cover every eventuality and employees, whatever their level of responsibility or role, must use their experience, skills and common sense when faced with aggression.

Special attention should be given in the guidelines to what is expected behaviour in the exceptional circumstances when physical restraint might be necessary. Potential risk situations should be anticipated and prepared for as far as possible.

Procedures: the following need to be considered:

- Is there a need for a detailed plan of the whereabouts and movements of all employees either inside the building or when out of the office on assignment? This might be especially necessary in high-risk employment, though any organization could find such a plan useful in an emergency such as a fire.
- Is a personal record kept which is readily available showing all visits, meetings, etc.?
- Is there periodic reporting in to base/supervisor/contact person as appropriate?
- Are there procedures for the assessment of potential or actual risk visits or customers/clients, in particular for informing superiors or colleagues? Are they made available?
- Is information made available on high-risk situations for all employees, but particularly for new and deputizing personnel? Good communication (both verbal and written) is essential in the workplace. Failure to share information is potentially dangerous. Risk and confrontation can be reduced by briefing employees as fully and regularly as possible. One person should be appointed to be responsible for this.

- Are extra precautions provided, such as accompanied visits, two-way radios, personal awareness alarms?
- Is there enhanced liaison with local police or other agencies?
- Are there special arrangements for the handling of cash?

Sexual harassment Management should be asked to adopt as policy the TUC Clause on Sexual Harassment:

> 'The Union and the Employer recognize the problem of sexual harassment in the workplace and are committed to ending it. Sexual harassment shall be defined as:
>
> 1 unnecessary touching or unwanted physical contact
> 2 suggestive remarks or other verbal abuse
> 3 leering at a person's body
> 4 compromising invitations
> 5 demands for sexual favours
> 6 physical assault
>
> Grievances under this clause will be handled with all possible speed and confidentiality. In settling the grievance, every effort will be made to discipline and relocate the harasser, not the victim.'

Training

Training in interpersonal skills plays a vital role in beating aggression in the workplace. All employees should be provided with appropriate courses and these should be attended by everyone together, so that both men and women fully understand the problems and difficulties either may face. In some cases it might be appropriate to run 'Women Only' courses on such topics as rape, but every effort should be made to counteract the notion that aggression is purely a women's problem.

The following questions might need to be answered:

- Do the existing training arrangements fully reflect the importance of the issue?
- What other courses would be appropriate? Do the courses offered cover the areas highlighted in this book? The Suzy Lamplugh Trust has a Training film made by Gower which is very helpful.
- Which member of staff is the nominated person responsible for ensuring that training in beating aggression has been given to all employees?
- Who is responsible for keeping a record of all those who receive training (and other specialist training) and for ensuring that retraining or refresher courses take place at appropriate intervals?

General environment

Management should be asked to acknowledge its responsibility to provide a workplace with easy access, good lighting and an inviting atmosphere. The following might be considered:

- Are security arrangements under constant review in order to highlight any alterations in working practice necessary to provide a safer working environment?
- Are alarm systems installed in places to which the public have access?
- Are telephone numbers of the emergency services and appropriate personnel displayed clearly, within easy access of all telephones?
- Is account taken of the fact that the design and layout of certain buildings sometimes place staff members in isolated and vulnerable positions? Are special safety measures taken?
- Public reception areas are particularly important. Are receptionists within easy access of other staff? Are interview rooms fitted out so that there is a calm atmosphere and also so as to enable occupants to achieve a swift exit should this become necessary?
- Is specific attention paid to street lighting and car-park facilities? (Multi-storey car parks can be both actual and perceived hazards, and this should be remembered especially if a firm is relocating.)
- If the general environment is identified as part of the problem, are steps taken such as the provision of taxis for late working, pressure on councils to provide adequate street lighting, etc.?

Support

In the event of a severe disturbance, police assistance will need to be summoned by the management. Summoning the police immediately after a violent incident promotes effective enquiries and enables the relevant persons to be interviewed. Everyone should support a police investigation when it proves necessary.

The following points need to be agreed:

- The employer should be committed to support any member of staff who is assaulted in the course of employment.
- Any person who assaults a member of staff during the course of his or her employment renders themselves liable to prosecution. Criminal assaults will be reported to the police. Where police action is not pursued the employer will support injured staff members who wish to pursue private action.

- A member of staff who has been assaulted in the course of employment should report the incident as soon as it is practicable and prepare a written report. Employees should seek guidance from their union or professional association at the same time.
- Where persistent threats are offered to a member of staff in the course of work, the employer will consider sending a written warning, informing the person concerned that legal action may be taken if a breach of the law occurs. On occasion the employer may have to apply for an injunction in the civil courts against individual clients.
- A senior member of staff should be available to accompany the worker to the police station and should remain with him or her during questioning and while statements are taken.
- A member of staff who suffers shock or injury should be encouraged to consult a doctor as soon as practicable and secure a medical statement of the injuries.
- Employees who have been victims of assault in the course of their employment should be given such leave of absence on full pay as is considered reasonable to take legal advice and appear in court, or consult with their trade union or professional body.

Implementation and monitoring

Issuing guidelines to staff members is a pointless exercise if they are not accessible and therefore not read. The same will occur if employers are not absolutely sure of their implications. Clearly, measures which are introduced need to be monitored for effectiveness; this will involve those who are most closely linked to their implementation. With any problem that needs solving, open discussion is an important basis from which to extract all the various strands. What may begin as an exercise to discuss a difficult and frightening issue can develop into a way of making life easier and better for everyone. A potentially depressing subject can become a platform to redefine good practice.

The dangers of procrastination

As with the open bow doors which caused the Zeebrugge ferry disaster, hindsight can be all too revealing. Lack of care, failing to bother, satisfaction with the status quo can leave an organization vulnerable. A very large employment agency recently consulted me on their safety measures for their staff. The personnel manager had sent out questionnaires to all their divisional directors and had received only a few replies. She confessed that she felt that as the agency had had such a good record over so long, most of the house staff could not raise much enthusiasm for taking on any new ideas.

As I read the reports I could see they showed a diversity of methods and ideas, and one or two felt that 'perhaps more could be done'. When I studied them more closely, I was considerably worried – for instance, two of the divisions were sending temporary secretaries to unknown clients in hotel rooms without any real checks being made. If there was a problem, not only might the girl suffer, but the whole agency's good name would be at risk.

Talking together, the personnel manager and I agreed that careful procedures can prevent tragedy and distress; an overtly caring organization gains a more confident and settled staff, and cared-for staff are more likely to work well, which must surely be the aim of any employer. We invited the divisional directors to a workshop and discussed the contents of this chapter. They brought together some excellent ideas which were easy to put into operation and applicable to their own situation. The core procedures were embroidered by additions which were particularly useful to each district. The time was considered very well spent and the personnel manager was very relieved with the results.

Endpiece

You may be like me and always judge a book by reading the opening sentence and then glancing at the back page before deciding whether it is worth buying. Just for *you* I decided I would be wise to add a postscript – a short piece which would direct you back to the beginning and assure you that all the topics and thoughts encapsulated in the titles on the Contents page are life skills of which you should take advantage. The learning of these could change your life or add value to it, not only at work but also every day.

The final chapter may seem dry and pedantic but it is essential to draw the attention of employers to their responsibilities for action against aggression, and to provide some ideas for you to give them to work on. It is up to you to ensure this does not go unnoticed. Aggression itself, especially in the workplace, seems to be a growing problem. Whether this is because we are more aware and also more determined to draw attention to abuse in its numerous forms – from verbal taunts to physical violence, sexual harassment to rape, innuendoes to assault – we will not fully know until our research is completed. But what I do want is increased reporting of statistics, so that even insurance companies take them seriously. It is up to you to speak up and make your voice heard.

At the same time, I hope the statistics will fall because you have learned and practised the relaxation and tension control techniques and acquired better skills of communication and assertion. I hope you will have studied and changed your attitudes and body language. I hope that you will be able to defuse and not provoke aggression, and deal with or alleviate danger. I hope you will learn how to avoid rather than confront risks or potential problems.

Reading this book should give you much to think about and probably even quite a lot of hard work. I trust you will take the view that you personally are more than worth the effort needed to acquire these skills of self-protection. I myself have no doubt that they are worthwhile.

When Suzy rang me on the Friday before that dark Monday when she totally disappeared from our lives, she told me with joy and excitement of all the things she was doing:

'Aren't you overdoing things rather a lot, darling?' I said.

'Come on, Mum,' she said. 'Life is for LIVING, don't forget that!'

I never have, and I now live with that thought in my heart. Life is for living, but real living needs quality; living with quality means living with freedom to choose, be ourselves and yet respect and value each other, whoever we may be. To be able to do this we need to live without harassment, danger and fear. This is why we need to take up the challenge of helping ourselves in all the ways we can, while continually urging those in authority to be aware and join our action against aggression. This will eventually benefit all of us.

We have always joked with our children, saying that they and all their friends seemed hell-bent on getting their BA – Been to America/ Africa/Australia/Asia – before setting out seriously to earn their living. I now think that BA should also stand for Beating Aggression. A rather insensitive reporter asked me recently if I didn't think that starting the Suzy Lamplugh Trust was rather like closing the stable door when the horse had bolted! Of course that is a fact I have to live with, and in the light of my daughter Suzy's disappearance I shall always wish we had understood the vital difference that Beating Aggression could have made to our lives. It is not too late for you to get *your* BA!

References

Adams, Frederick and Webster, Gillian, *Hands Off! Hap-ki-do Self-Defence for Women*, Jarrold Colour Publications, Norwich, 1986

Alberti, Robert and Emmons, Michael, *Your Perfect Right: A Guide to Assertive Living*, Impact Books, London, 5th edition 1986

Ashworth, Henry, *Assertiveness at Work*, McGraw-Hill, New York, 1981

Ball, May, 'Training to be Assertive', *The Lamp* 42.1, February 1985, pp. 31–35

Barlow, Geoffrey, *Video Violence and Children*, Hodder & Stoughton, London, 1985

Berne, Eric, *Games People Play*, Penguin, London, 1967

Bond, Meg, 'The Art of Relaxation', *Nursing Mirror*, 6 October 1982, pp. 38–40

Bond, Meg, 'Assertiveness in District Nursing', *Journal of District Nursing*, February 1985, pp. 22–25

Bond, Meg, 'Being Assertive', Managing Care Pack 18, Distance Learning Centre, Polytechnic of the South Bank, London, 1987

Bond, Meg, 'Dare You Say No?', *Nursing Mirror*, 13 October 1982, pp. 40–43

Bond, Meg, 'Do You Care About Your Colleagues?', *Nursing Mirror*, 20 October 1982, pp. 42–44

Bond, Meg, *Stress and Self-Awareness: A Guide for Nurses*, Heinemann Nursing, London, 1986

Bond, Meg and Kilty, James, 'Practical Methods of Dealing with Stress', Human Potential Research Project, University of Surrey, 1982

Brain, Paul, *Alcohol and Aggression*, Croom Helm, London, 1986

Brown, Robert; Bute, Stanley and Ford, Peter, *Social Workers at Risk: The Prevention and Management of Violence*, Macmillan Education Ltd, London, 1986

Buss, A. H., *The Psychology of Aggression*, Wiley, New York, 1961

Buss, A. H., *Psychopathology*, Wiley, New York, 1966

Bute, Stanley, 'Guidelines for Coping with Violence by Clients', *Social Work Today* vol. 15, 1979, pp. 13–15

Butler, Pamela, *Self-Assertion for Women*, Harper & Row, New York, 1981

Cambridgeshire Councy Council Social Services Department, 'Guidelines for the Management of Violence at Work', 1986

Cambridgeshire County Council Social Services Department, 'Management of Violence at Work: Guidelines for Social Services Staff', May 1987

Camden Council Social Services, 'Guidelines on Violence towards Staff', August 1986

Clutterbuck, David, 'When Sex Harassment Becomes More Than a Bawdy Office Joke', *International Management*, March 1981, pp. 10–14

Consumer Association, *Living With Stress: The 'Which' Report*, Consumer Association, London, 1981

Cooper, Cary L., *The Stress Check: Coping With the Stresses of Life and Work*, Spectrum Books, Prentice-Hall Inc, New Jersey, 1981

Cox, Tom, *Stress*, Macmillan Education Ltd, London, 1978

Davidson, Marilyn and Cooper, Cary L., *Stress and the Woman Manager*, Martin Robertson, London, 1983

Dickson, Anne, *A Woman in Your Own Right: Assertiveness and You*, Quartet, London, 1982

Dobson, C. R., *Stress: The Hidden Adversary*, Lancaster MTP Press, Lancaster, 1982

Elle Magazine research into Danger for Women at Work, June 1987

Fensterheim, Herbert and Baer, Jean, *Don't Say Yes When You Want to Say No*, Futura, London, 1985

Freudenberger, Herbert J., 'Staff Burn-out', *Journal of Social Issues* 30.1, 1974, pp. 159–65

Galessi and Galessi, *Assert Yourself: How to Be Your Own Person*, Human Sciences Press, London, 1977

Hadjifoliou, Nathalie, *Women and Harassment at Work*, Pluto Press, London, 1983

Handy, Charles, *Understanding Organisations*, Penguin, London, 1976

'Harassment at Work', *Equal Opportunities Review* 4, November–December 1985, pp. 8–11

Hargie, O.; Saunders, C. and Dickson, D., *Social Skills in Interpersonal Communication*, Croom Helm, London, 1983

Hemming, Heather, 'Sexual Harassment in Britain', *Equal Opportunities International* 4(4), 1985, pp. 5–9

Heron, John, 'Behaviour Analysis in Education and Training', Human Potential Research Project, University of Surrey, 1977

Holland, Stevie, 'Stress in Nursing', Distance Learning Centre, Polytechnic of the South Bank, London, 1987

Holmes, Sue, 'Stress and Nutrition', *Nursing Times*, 19 September 1984, pp. 53–55

Howells, Lynne, 'Dealing with Aggression: An Awareness Programme', Women's Unit, Birmingham City Council, 1986

Hoyman, Michele and Robinson, Ronda, 'Interpreting the New Sexual Harassment Guidelines', *Personnel Journal* 59 (12), December 1980, pp. 996–1000

Hunter, Catherine, 'Easing the Tension', *Nursing Times*, 16 January 1985

Hyett, Ken, 'How to Escape the Time Trap', *Nursing Times*, 16 January 1985, pp. 32–34

IDS, 'Sexual Harassment at Work', IDS Brief 282, August 1984, i–iv (Employment law briefing: 69)

Kilty, James, 'Self and Peer Assessment', Human Potential Research Project, University of Surrey, 1978

Kilty, James and Boud, David, 'Self and Peer Assessment for Educational Staff Development: A Workshop Facilitator's Guide', Tertiary Education Research Centre, University of New South Wales, 1978

Lamplugh, Diana, 'Slimnastics', *Stress Medicine* vol. 1, 1985, pp. 1–6

Lamplugh, Diana and Nottidge, Pamela, *The New Penguin Slimnastics: A Guide to Good Living*, Penguin, London, 1980

Lamplugh, Diana and Nottidge Pamela, *Slimnastics: The Whole Person Approach to Fitness*, Oxford Illustrated Press, London, 1984

Lazarus, Richard S., *Patterns of Adjustment*, McGraw-Hill, New York, 1976

Lazarus, Richard S., *Psychological Stress and the Coping Process*, McGraw-Hill, New York, 1966

Leap, Terry and Gray, Edmund, 'Corporate Responsibility in Cases of Sexual Harassment', *Business Horizons* 23, 1–5 October 1980, pp. 58–65

Leeds Trade Union and Community Resource and Information

Centre, 'Sexual Harassment of Women at Work: A Study from West Yorkshire', TUCRIC (funded by the Equal Opportunities Commission), Leeds, 1983

Lindenfield, Gail, *Assert Yourself: A Self-Help Programme in Assertiveness Training for Groups and Individuals, Men and Women*, self-published, London, 1986 (available from Changes Bookshop, London NW6)

Linenberger, Patricia and Keaveney, Timothy J., 'Sexual Harassment: The Employer's Legal Obligations', *Personnel: The Management of People at Work*, November–December 1981, pp. 60–68

London Borough of Hackney, 'Recommendations for the Organisation of Personal Security Measures for Field Officers', 1986

London Borough of Haringey Social Services Department, 'Guidelines to Staff to Assist in the Management of Aggressive Behaviour by Clients or Members of the Public', June 1986

McCormack, Arlene, 'The Sexual Harassment of Students by Teachers: The Case of Students in Science', *Sex Roles* 13 (1–2), July 1985, pp. 21–32

McGuigan, F. J.; Sime, W. E. and Wallace, J., *Stress and Tension Control*, Plenium Publishing Corporation, New York, 1980

Madders, Jane, *Stress and Relaxation*, Martin Dunitz, London, 1982

Martin, David, 'Sexual Harassment at Work: A Legal View', *Industrial Management and Data Systems*, January–February 1984, pp. 11–15

Maslow, A. H., 'Self-Actualisation and Beyond' in *Challenges of Humanistic Psychology* (ed. Bugentall, J. E. T.), McGraw-Hill, New York, 1967, pp. 279–86

Menzies, Isabel, 'A Case Study for the Functioning of Social Systems as Defence Against Anxiety', *Human Relationships* 13 (2), 1960, pp. 95–123, 209–20

Meyer, Mary Coeli *et al.*, *Sexual Harassment: What Is It, How Prevalent Is It, Why Is Understanding It So Important, What are the Legal Consequences?*, Petrocelli, New York, 1981

Minors, David; Waterhouse, James and Folkard, Simon, 'Out of Rhythm', *Nursing Times*, 10 April 1985, pp. 26–27

Mitchell, L., *Simple Relaxation*, John Murray, London, 1981

Morris, Desmond, *Manwatching*, Jonathan Cape, London, 1979

NALGO, 'Coping with Violence at Work', *NALGO News*, 27 September 1985

NALGO, 'Sexual Harassment is a Trade Union Issue', NALGO, London, 1981

Nottidge, Pamela and Lamplugh, Diana, *Slimnastics*, Angus & Robertson, London, 1970

Nottidge, Pamela and Lamplugh, Diana, *Stress and Overstress*, Angus & Robertson, London, 1970 (republished as *The Commonsense Guide to Stress Control*, Slimnastics Books, London, 1982)

Open University, Health Education Council and Scottish Health Education Group, *The Good Health Guide*, Harper & Row, New York, 1980

Orr, Jean, 'Managing Aggression', Distance Learning Centre, Polytechnic of the South Bank, London, 1987

Orwell, George, *1984*, Penguin, London, 1948

Poyner, Barry and Warne, Caroline, 'Violence to Staff: A Basis for Assessment and Prevention', Tavistock Institute of Human Relations, HMSO, London, 1986

Quinn, Kaleghi, *Stand Your Ground*, Orbis, London, 1983

Rahe, Richard, *The Sunday Times Book of Body Maintenance*, Times Newspapers, London, 1978

Read, Sue, *Sexual Harassment at Work: Is It Just Fun and Games?*, Hamlyn, London, 1982

The Reebok Guide to Safe Running, Reebok UK Ltd in conjunction with The Suzy Lamplugh Trust, London, 1987

Renick, James C., 'Sexual Harassment at Work: Why It Happens, What to Do About It', *Personnel Journal* 59 (8), August 1980, pp. 658–62

Rogers, C. R., *Carl Rogers on Personal Power*, Pocket Books, New York, 1977

Rowe, Mary P., 'Dealing With Sexual Harassment', *Harvard Business Review*, May–June 1981, pp. 42–46

Seddon, Vickey, 'Keeping Women in their Place', *Marxism Today*, July 1983, pp. 20–23

Sedley, Ann and Benn, Melissa, 'Sexual Harassment at Work', National Council for Civil Liberties, London, 1982

Selye, Hans, *The Stress of Life*, McGraw-Hill, New York, 1956

'Sexual Harassment at Work', *Labour Research* 72 (9), September 1982, pp. 234–35

Smith, Manuel, *When I Say No, I Feel Guilty*, Dial Press, London, 1975

Stanko, Elizabeth, *Intimate Intrusions: Women's Experience of Male Violence*, Routledge and Kegan Paul, London, 1985

Stasz, Clarice, 'Sexual Harassment', *Queen's Quarterly* 87 (3), 1980, pp. 481–84

Stones, Rosemary, *Too Close Encounters and What to Do about Them*, Methuen Children's Books Ltd, London, 1987

Strathclyde Regional Council, Social Work Department, 'Violence to Staff: Policies and Procedures', January 1986

Strechert, Kathryn, *The Credibility Gap*, Thorous, New York, 1987

Townend, Anni, 'Assertion Training: A Handbook for Those in Training', Family Planning Association, London, 1984

Trades Union Congress, 'Sexual Harassment at Work', TUC Guide and Workplace Programme for Trade Unionists, February 1985

Transport and General Workers Union, 'Combating Sexual Harassment: TGWU Shop Stewards' Handbook', TGWU, London, 1984

Turton, Pat and Orr, Jean, *Learning to Care in the Community*, Hodder & Stoughton, London, 1985

Tutt, Norman, *Violence*, HMSO, London, 1976

Tysoe, Maryon, 'The Sexual Harassers', *New Society*, 4 November 1982

Vance, Connie, 'On Becoming a Professional', *Nurse Educator* 10.3, May–June 1985, pp. 20–25

'Violence to Staff in the Health Services', *Health Services Advisory Committee Report*, HMSO, London, 1987

Wallfesh, Sue, 'Sexual Harassment and How You React to It', *Horoscope*, September 1981, pp. 12–14

Walmsley, Roy, 'Personal Violence', Home Office Research Study 89, HMSO, London, 1986

WEA/HEC, *Women and Health*, WEA, London, 1987

Wilson, Elizabeth, *What Is to Be Done About Violence Against Women*, Penguin, London, 1983

Wyre, Ray, *Women, Men and Rape*, Perry Publications, Oxford, 1986